KNOW. CHOOSE. GIVE.

A Practical Guide for
Personal & Professional
Success Using the
Six Seconds Emotional
Intelligence Framework

Dr. Liza D. Johnson, Ed.D.

Participant Workbook

sixseconds
THE EMOTIONAL INTELLIGENCE NETWORK

Know, Choose, Give: A practical guide for personal & professional success using the
Six Seconds emotional intelligence framework - Participant Workbook
Copyright ©2020 Six Seconds, Liza D. Johnson
Published by Six Seconds

PO Box 1985
Freedom, CA 95019
Web: www.6seconds.org
Email: staff@6seconds.org
Phone: (831) 763-1800

All rights reserved. No part of this publication may be reproduced or distributed in any form or by any means, or stored in a database or retrieval system, without the prior written permission of the publisher.

ISBN: 978-1-935667-48-3

Printed in China

License For Use
Any use of this material means the user has read and agreed to the Publisher's Terms of Use (6sec.org/terms) and Privacy Policy (6sec.org/privacy). Subject to these terms, the purchaser of this work is licensed to utilize the contents of this program provided that (a) a new copy of the Participant Workbook is purchased for each and every participant (student) utilizing these materials, whether this curriculum is used in whole or in part; (b) that those delivering this curriculum are educational professionals with appropriate training and qualification to do so.

Limit of Liability / Disclaimer of Warranty
While the publisher and author have used their best efforts in preparing this book, they disclaim any implied warranties of merchantability or fitness for a particular purpose. The advice in this book may not be suitable for your situation. You agree to consult with a professional where appropriate. Neither the publisher nor author shall be liable for any loss of profit or any other damages, including but not limited to special, incidental, consequential, or other damages. In any case the maximum liability shall be equal to the retail price of this book.

By using this book you agree to these terms; if you do not agree return this book unread to the publisher for a full refund.

This book includes models and excerpts ©Six Seconds, Used by permission, including the Six Seconds Model and definitions, TFA Model, What-How-Why Model, 123KCG, and Feeling Log. The Plutchik Model reprinted by permission of American Scientist, magazine of Sigma Xi, The Scientific Research Society.

Welcome to Six Seconds

Six Seconds was founded in 1997 as a nonprofit organization dedicated to **supporting people to create positive change**. Six Seconds believes the world would be a better place if a billion people were practicing the skills of emotional intelligence (EQ). Six Seconds researches and shares scientific, global, transformational tools and methods to support that goal. With offices and representatives in 25 countries and members in 167 countries, their community extends around the globe. From schools where children love to learn, to corporations where people thrive, to programs rebuilding lives, Six Seconds' solutions are life-changing – and empower people to take ownership of a positive future.

About Six Seconds

At a Glance…

What?

…501(c)3 not-for-profit helps people learn emotional intelligence

Why?

…EQ improves leadership, learning, effectiveness, communication, relationships, and health

How?

…Research, training, assessment tools, curricula, world-wide network

Who?

…Corporations, government agencies, schools, community organizations

Website: www.6seconds.org

The Six Seconds Model of EQ

The Six Seconds model turns emotional intelligence (EQ) theory into practice for your personal and professional life.

EQ is the capacity to blend thinking and feeling to make optimal decisions — which is key to having a successful relationship with yourself and others. EQ is a learnable, measurable, scientifically validated skillset that fuels better effectiveness, relationships, wellbeing and quality of life – for adults and children. To provide a practical and simple way to learn and practice EQ, Six Seconds developed a three-part model in 1997 as a process – an action plan for using EQ in daily life.

This model of EQ-in-Action begins with three important pursuits to become more aware (noticing what you do), more intentional (doing what you mean), and more purposeful (doing it for a reason). We call the three pursuits: Know Yourself, Choose Yourself, and Give Yourself. We will discuss this more in-depth as part of a lesson in the workbook.

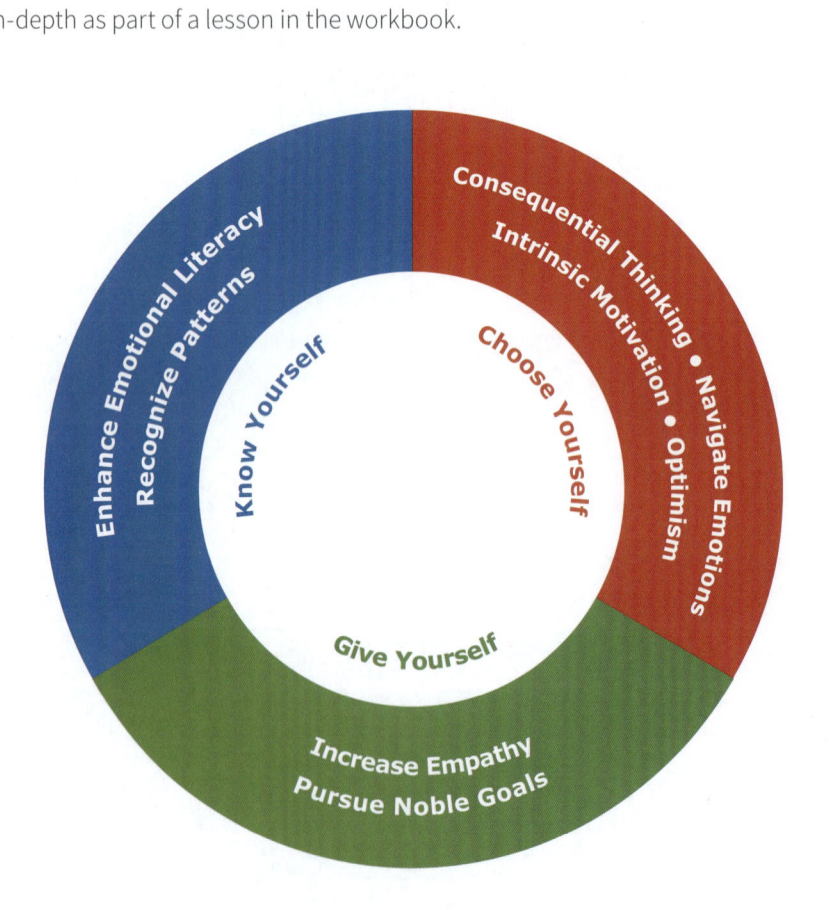

About the Author

Dr. Liza D. Johnson is the Director of a campus-wide emotional intelligence (EQ) program and Assistant Director to the President at the University of Dubuque located in Dubuque, Iowa, USA. In the last 14 years, Johnson has worked in the education field and is strongly committed to educating and forming the whole child. She created, teaches, and directs an EQ undergraduate college course that fulfills a general education requirement. This experiential course helps students develop and apply critical skills necessary to be successful in making sustained and positive change.

Johnson leads 40+ trained faculty and staff members who either teach the undergraduate course and/or infuse EQ in their specialized areas on campus. She is passionate about paving the way for the integration of EQ into all campus operations at the higher education level in meaningful and effective ways.

In addition, Dr. Johnson is working closely with the Dubuque Community Schools, police, and city government on a community-wide implementation plan of EQ. In 2019, she joined the Six Seconds team as an EQ Ambassador to help fulfill their mission of gathering one billion people to practice EQ.

Her educational background includes B.A. in Psychology, M.A in School Counseling, M.A. in Organizational Management, and Ed.D. in Educational Leadership.

Why EQ?

Freedman & Roitman (2019) remarked in *The EQ Gym Workbook,*

"We live in turbulent times. There is so much complexity. Stress is rising. We have incredible technology to communicate with each other, yet people feel more and more isolated. This combination makes people more volatile, more impatient, more likely to fight, flee, or freeze. This makes it harder to solve the real problems we face individually and collectively.

The emotional challenge is growing – around the world, at work, at home. Even children are experiencing greater distress. Maybe once-upon-a-time there was little need to actively learn the skills of emotional intelligence. In this world of growing complexity, however, we all need to develop more insight and skill to handle our own and others' emotions effectively and to be better prepared for the future. That's where emotional intelligence comes in.

There's a growing body of research showing that the skills of emotional intelligence help people...

Achieve more effective results

Be and feel healthier

Make better decisions

Form stronger relationships

Young people with high EQ earn higher grades, stay in school, and make healthier choices. Adults with high EQ have better career advancement, are more effective leaders and salespeople, and have better personal & professional relationships."

A Critical Need for EQ in Higher Education

For many years, college curricula focused on the academic skills of education whereas other life skills were often missing from student learning experiences. In present-day higher education, traditional academic subjects are systematically taught and tested, but grit, empathy, responsibility, and self-regulation are not routinely addressed in undergraduate curricula. Emotional intelligence (EQ) is the critical missing link to student success across institutions.

It is clear there are a variety of demanding issues and stressors that college students need to cope with in order to navigate college successfully. They may face a number of unfavorable outcomes such as homesickness, anxiety, stress, relationship issues, depression, and failure.

By educating college students on EQ competencies, such as healthy ways to cope and navigate stress, students will possess the appropriate tools and strategies to alleviate or combat some of these tough issues. EQ provides a way to create effective and healthy coping skills. "Overall, emotional intelligence is currently evaluated as being an important and valuable potential personal resource for students in school settings" (Zeidner & Matthews, 2018, p. 103). EQ is a powerful framework that allows institutions to advance students' success and improve their quality of life.

Effectively integrating EQ in higher education, students will be educated on how to make more meaningful and productive life choices. EQ is critical to students' retention and engagement, overall wellbeing, and professional success beyond college.

A Critical Need for EQ in Businesses & Organizations

Freedman & Roitman (2019) remarked in *The EQ Gym Workbook,*

"EQ seems to be useful for individuals, but is it really crucial for organizations? Why?

In the last 20 years there has been extensive research about this question.

From American Express to Google, businesses have begun to embrace the concept. Harvard Business Review calls it "the key to professional success." Schools, hospitals, and government agencies world-wide are adopting EQ practices. From elementary school students to army officers, a curriculum of emotional awareness is providing a new perspective on people.

Looking at one of the most recent studies:

- In the 2017 Vitality Report led by Six Seconds, leaders and team members in 95 countries answered the question: "Is emotional intelligence development a priority in your organization?" They also answered questions about performance in four KPIs (key performance indicators): Retention, Productivity, Customer Focus, and Future Success.

- Organizations where emotional intelligence development is a priority are 22 times as likely to be high performers on the 4 KPIs (which are Retention, Productivity, Customer Focus, and Future Success). To put that in perspective: People who smoke cigarettes are 8 times as likely to get cancer.

- Frustration seems to be the word-of-the-year at work – and equipping people with skills to be "smarter with feelings" may be essential in this context."

Your EQ Journey

Welcome to your EQ journey! We are inviting you to participate in *Know, Choose, Give: A practical guide for personal & professional success using the Six Seconds emotional intelligence framework*. Your success at improving your EQ will be determined by how much you practice and apply the concepts we explore.

In this course, you will....

- Strengthen your own emotional intelligence.
- Understand the power of Know Yourself, Choose Yourself, Give Yourself (KCG) model and approach to increasing and applying EQ.

- Participate in various EQ exercises to practice the skill of EQ.
- Learn tools to help strengthen and build your relationships with others.
- Engage in a wide range of additional resources by visiting 6sec.org/kcgp.

This course is more than merely learning about EQ, it is about living EQ. We want EQ to be an authentic and strong component of your daily life. To do this, it requires persistence, hard work, and dedication. While this program includes many tools for developing EQ, your motivation towards practicing and setting personal goals will be critical to your success. The more you practice EQ, the better you become at EQ.

Therefore, there are various opportunities in this workbook to dive into self-discovery and set personal goals towards developing your EQ. Setting goals is essential to success and achievement. At Six Seconds, we use the technique called C.L.E.A.R. goals developed by Dr. Anabel L. Jensen, co-founder of Six Seconds, to set and achieve well-formed goals.

Most of us are familiar with the S.M.A.R.T. process of goal setting to ensure that our goals are:

- **Specific** – direct, detailed, and meaningful
- **Measurable** – quantifiable to track progress and success
- **Achievable** – realistic and resources needed are attainable
- **Relevant** – aligns with our purpose, values, and mission
- **Timed** – timeline is established

The S.M.A.R.T. process has brought success for many. In fact, a Dominican University of California study in 2007 found that the goals that are specifically identified, written down and shared with a friend are far more successful than those without written goals. People are most effective with accountability, written commitment and peer support.

However, Dr. Anabel L. Jensen added something important to the S.M.A.R.T. process. She emphasized what she considered to be missing: the *human* and *emotional* sides of how we get things done. She focused on three aspects to add:

- **Reward** yourself for achieving the goal, especially if it's a major milestone
- **Recognize** the contributions of those who helped (often neglected)
- **Celebrate** the achievement together

The C.L.E.A.R. goals are in harmony with EQ. They will help boost your effectiveness by providing a sense of direction and purpose in reaching your EQ goals. Emotionally intelligent goal setting should include these five concepts:

- **Collaborate:** emotionally intelligent goal-setting should include all of the stakeholders and elicit their opinions, theories, tactics and other ideas to help bring the goal to fruition
- **Listen:** be open to all ideas and have a collaborative mindset
- **Empathy:** empathize with others and search for ways to compromise between what you *want* and what is *possible*
- **Adapt:** make your goals realistic for the environment you are in
- **Reward:** celebrate your achievements in a way that fuels your internal motivation

By remembering that we are not working with machines (or systems, processes, or assets), but with people, we can bring a compassionate humanism to goal setting and create objectives which are supported and realistic, and which energize the people around us.

For more information on C.L.E.A.R. goals, visit 6sec.org/a/clear

Supporting Positive Change

"Change is the end result of all true learning" –Leo Buscaglia

As a community of changemakers contributing to a world filled with insight, connection, and purpose, at Six Seconds we agree with Buscaglia. What is learning? It is a process of change. It starts at a neurological level, neurons rewiring, and cascades into global transformation.

We all have an opportunity to change and strive to be a better person, if we choose to. What is it you want to change or make better? *Know, Choose, Give: A practical guide for personal & professional success using the Six Seconds' emotional intelligence framework* will empower you to make intentional choices that will lead to powerful results. When we choose to embrace positive change, personal transformation is possible. During this course, genuinely invest in yourself. By doing so, you will create a more promising future.

Depending on your view of change, it can either keep you stagnate or facilitate remarkable growth and personal development. Therefore, we believe it is important to identify three myths associated with change, they are:

- Myth #1: change is a solo act. Instead, change often involves another stakeholder, even if it's only for support or resources.

- Myth #2: change is rational. Instead, change is often an emotional process and the obstacles and unproductive coping strategies are coupled with emotions.

- Myth #3: change is linear. Rather, research has shown change is dynamic. So small hiccups or setbacks do not mean failure; they are to be expected and prepared for.

Reeducating our minds on change can help us move forward towards solutions. At Six Seconds, we focus on developing EQ skills, not just for the sake of having high EQ, but to actually support positive change. Research developed by Six Seconds suggests that EQ can make us more successful in the areas of effectiveness, relationships, life satisfaction, and wellbeing. We invite you to actively participate in the workbook to both increase your EQ and support positive change within your life and others.

> "Our feelings are
> our most genuine paths
> to knowledge."
>
> – Audré Lorde

Contents

Course Learning Outcomes 13

INTRODUCTION 17
Ground Rules 19
Emotional Intelligence (EQ) 21
Powerful Questions 27

CHAPTER 1: KNOW YOURSELF 31
Check-in 33
Thoughts 41
Feelings & Emotions 43
State of Mind 47
Core Values 53
Core Beliefs 57
Self-Confidence 61
Think, Feel, & Act (TFA) 65
Know Yourself Strategies 71
Know Yourself Goal Setting 72

CHAPTER 2: CHOOSE YOURSELF 73
Pessimism 75
Optimism 77
Emotional Regulation 79
Anger 83
Fear 87
Positive Self-Talk 91
Negative Self-Talk 95
Stress Tolerance 99
Gratitude 103

Contents

Grit 107
Problem Solving With EQ 111
Consequential Thinking 115
Responsibility Taking 119
Impulse Control 123
Positive Self-Interest (PSI) 127
Choose Yourself Strategies 131
Choose Yourself Goal Setting 132

CHAPTER 3: GIVE YOURSELF 133
Empathy 135
Healthy Relationships 139
Emotional Expression 145
Feedback 151
Independence 161
Communication Styles 167
Problem Ownership 171
Negotiation 175
Conflict Management 179
Noble Goal 183
Give Yourself Strategies 187
Give Yourself Goal Setting 188

CHAPTER 4: POSITIVE ACTION PLAN 189
Positive Action Plan 191
Invitation 193
Special Thank You 195
References 197
Gratitude Journal 201

COURSE LEARNING OUTCOMES

Six Seconds EQ Model	Six Seconds Competency	Know. Choose. Give. Concept	Outcomes (Learners Will Be Able To . . .)
		Emotional Intelligence (EQ)	Identify Know Choose Give (KCG) and its significance. Recognize that EQ is critical to success.
		Powerful Questions	Identify powerful questions and their significance. Recognize that powerful questions are critical to personal growth and development. Engage in the creation and pursuit of powerful questions throughout this course and beyond.
Know Yourself	Enhance Emotional Literacy	Check-in	Identify check-in and its significance. Participate in check-in using feeling words and understand connection to actions. Recognize various techniques to utilize during check-in with self and others.
	Recognize Patterns	Thoughts	Identify thoughts and their significance. Demonstrate awareness of their own thoughts.
	Enhance Emotional Literacy	Feelings & Emotions	Identify feelings and emotions and their significance. Demonstrate awareness of their own feelings and emotions.
	Recognize Patterns	State of Mind	Identify state of mind and its significance. Identify their own state of mind in various situations. Recognize ways to control their own state of mind.
	Recognize Patterns	Core Values	Identify core values and its significance. Identify their own core values. Recognize ways to make their core values fully present in their lives.
	Recognize Patterns	Core Beliefs	Identify core beliefs and their significance. Recognize their own empowering and limiting beliefs. Analyze the impact of these beliefs.
	Recognize Patterns	Self-Confidence	Identify self-confidence and its significance. Recognize their own strengths. Recognize new ways to use their own strengths to help in relationships and personal success.
	Recognize Patterns	Think, Feel, & Act (TFA)	Identify Think, Feel, and Act (TFA) and its significance. Identify and explain their own thoughts, feelings, and actions using the TFA tool. Recognize ways to become more intentional versus reactional using the TFA tool.

Six Seconds EQ Model	Six Seconds Competency	Know. Choose. Give. Concept	Outcomes (Learners Will Be Able To . . .)
Choose Yourself	Recognize Patterns	Pessimism	Identify pessimism and its significance. Recognize and analyze their pessimistic styles of thinking and feeling.
	Exercising Optimism	Optimism	Identify optimism and its significance. Recognize and analyze their optimistic styles of thinking and feeling. Apply a proactive perspective of hope and possibility.
	Navigate Emotions	Emotional Regulation	Identify emotional regulation and its significance. Demonstrate methods to regulate their own emotions to benefit self and others. Apply the "Stop, Think, Choose" method to practice emotional regulation.
	Navigate Emotions	Anger	Identify anger and its significance. Recognize their own warning signs associated with anger. Demonstrate awareness of their own feelings that precede anger. Demonstrate methods to manage anger.
	Navigate Emotions	Fear	Identify fear and its significance. Recognize the impact fear has on self. Practice changing thoughts to manage fear.
	Navigate Emotions	Positive Self-Talk	Identify positive self-talk and its significance. Generate and use affirmations and solution-focused statements.
	Navigate Emotions	Negative Self-Talk	Identify negative self-talk and its significance. Identify their own negative self-talk and reframe to positive self-talk.
	Navigate Emotions	Stress Tolerance	Identify stress tolerance and its significance. Identify how they experience stress. Recognize methods to reduce their ongoing and daily stress.
	Exercise Optimism	Gratitude	Identify gratitude and its significance. Demonstrate gratitude in a reflective and written form to oneself and others.
	Engage Intrinsic Motivation	Grit	Identify grit and its significance. Measure their own level of grit. Identify ways to build, improve, and increase grit.
	Navigate Emotions	Problem Solving with EQ	Identify problem solving with EQ and its significance. Recognize that emotions influence one's problem solving abilities. Apply KCG to solve problems effectively.

Six Seconds EQ Model	Six Seconds Competency	Know. Choose. Give. Concept	Outcomes (Learners Will Be Able To . . .)
Choose Yourself	Apply Consequential Thinking	Consequential Thinking	Identify consequential thinking and its significance. Practice if/then thinking and select alternatives that lead to an optimistic state of mind.
	Engage Intrinsic Motivation	Responsibility Taking	Identify responsibility taking and its significance. Determine level of responsibility in their own life and analyze the impact of blaming self and others.
	Navigate Emotions	Impulse Control	Identify impulse control and its significance. Determine level of impulse control in their own life and analyze the impact. Demonstrate strategies to manage their impulses.
	Engage Intrinsic Motivation	Positive Self-Interest (PSI)	Identify PSI and its significance. Recognize ways to include PSI in their own life. Identify ways to overcome challenges in practicing PSI in their own life.
Give Yourself	Increase Empathy	Empathy	Identify empathy and its significance. Recognize and apply skills that will increase empathy.
	Increase Empathy	Healthy Relationships	Identify a healthy relationship and its significance. Recognize healthy and unhealthy relationships in their own life. Reflect how they express love and appreciation in relationships.
	Increase Empathy	Emotional Expression	Identify emotional expression and its significance. Recognize emotional expressions in self and others. Analyze their emotional expression through social media.
	Increase Empathy	Feedback	Identify feedback and its significance. Recognize difference between feedback and criticism. Demonstrate ability to use "I" statements for feedback and in response to criticism.
	Pursue Noble Goal	Independence	Identify independence and its significance. Recognize difference between independent and dependent actions and their consequences. Determine level of independence in their own life.
	Increase Empathy	Communication Styles	Identify communication styles and their significance. Recognize the communication styles they use and the impact they have on others.

Six Seconds EQ Model	Six Seconds Competency	Know. Choose. Give. Concept	Outcomes (Learners Will Be Able To . . .)
Give Yourself	Pursue Noble Goal	Problem Ownership	Identify problem ownership and its significance. Analyze situations to determine problem ownership. Identify appropriate skills for the problem situation (i.e. empathy, reflective listening, "I" statements).
	Pursue Noble Goal	Negotiation	Identify negotiation and its significance. Recognize and apply steps to successfully negotiate with others.
	Pursue Noble Goal	Conflict Management	Identify conflict management and its significance. Recognize their own conflict management style and the impact it has on others. Apply skills to effectively manage conflict.
	Pursue Noble Goals	Noble Goal	Identify Noble Goal and its significance. Create their own Noble Goal. Recognize ways to use their Noble Goal to connect their daily choices with their overarching sense of purpose.

INTRODUCTION

Notes

GROUND RULES

To ensure that we act as empowered individuals, we will follow these guidelines for actions:

Notes

EMOTIONAL INTELLIGENCE

What is Emotional Intelligence (EQ)?

EQ is the ability to recognize our emotions and other people's emotions along with the ability to use this awareness to become intentional and purposeful. EQ is a learnable, measurable, scientifically validated skillset that fuels better effectiveness, relationships, wellbeing and quality of life – for adults and children.

The Six Seconds model of EQ-in-Action, known as KCG, has three parts:

- **Know Yourself (Awareness):** The ability to clearly seeing what I feel and do. This is when I check-in with myself and ask, What am I feeling?

Know Yourself gives the "what" – When we practice Know Yourself, we know our strengths and challenges, we know what we are doing, what we want, and what to change. Knowing Yourself includes awareness and insight about our thoughts, our emotions and our actions. Having insight includes recognizing the causes and effects of our own feelings and reactions. It's like investigating, experimenting, observing, and interpreting ourselves with curiosity. Part of Know Yourself is not only recognizing but acknowledging our habits and patterns. So knowing ourselves requires self-honesty: accepting our own qualities and faults, our own experiences and emotions, and our own power.

- **Choose Yourself (Management):** The ability to pause, take a deep breath in order to evaluate my options. This is when I check-in with myself and ask, What choices do I have?

Choose Yourself provides the "how" – When we practice Choose Yourself, we know how to take action, how to influence ourselves and others, and how to make a proactive response and make a new choice. In Choose Yourself, we first PAUSE the initial reaction so we are able to make a new choice. In this step, we also consider different options, risks and benefits and opportunities. We learn we can choose our emotions and navigate them to become more intentional versus reactional.

- **Give Yourself (Direction):** The ability to understand what's really important to me. This is when I check-in with myself and ask, What do I really want?

Give Yourself delivers the "why" – when we practice Give Yourself we are clear on why to respond a certain way, why to move in a new direction, and why others should come on board. All three

EMOTIONAL INTELLIGENCE

areas of KCG are required to make change, to grow. And without the Give Yourself part, without the clear WHY, it's impossible to sustain in the long-term. This is especially important when we're caught in conflict or struggle. When we're reacting (fighting, fleeing, or freezing) to protect our egos and feel comfortable, it's easy to think only of the short-term. Instead, if we can shift over to Give Yourself we step out of the short-term survival mode and remember what's most important to us.

Why is emotional intelligence important?

We live in an ever changing, fast-paced, and technology-focused world. We are connected online 24/7, however people are feeling more isolated and stressed. This is affecting people's abilities, relationships with others, and overall wellbeing. We need to develop critical skills to be able to navigate today's challenges. This is where EQ comes in.

Today, "there is growing evidence that [emotional intelligence] EI significantly contributes to both occupational and educational performance and it is not surprising that there have been calls that universities and colleges need to provide programming to develop or enhance EI-related competencies" (Brackett, Rivers, & Salovey, 2019).

According to Bradberry & Greaves (2009) in Emotional Intelligence 2.0, "EQ is the foundation for a host of critical personal and interpersonal skills—it impacts almost everything we say and do each day. EQ is the single biggest predictor of success in the workplace and the strongest driver of leadership and personal excellence."

EMOTIONAL INTELLIGENCE

Suppose I decide it's time to make a change in life…

…if I am strong in **Know Yourself,** I will see *what* to change because I've got the clarity from my emotions and recognize my patterns.

…if I am strong in **Choose Yourself,** I will actually know *how* to make the change by pausing and redirecting- responding instead of reacting.

…if I am strong in **Give Yourself,** I will see *why* I need to make the change because of my connection with others and clarity of purpose.

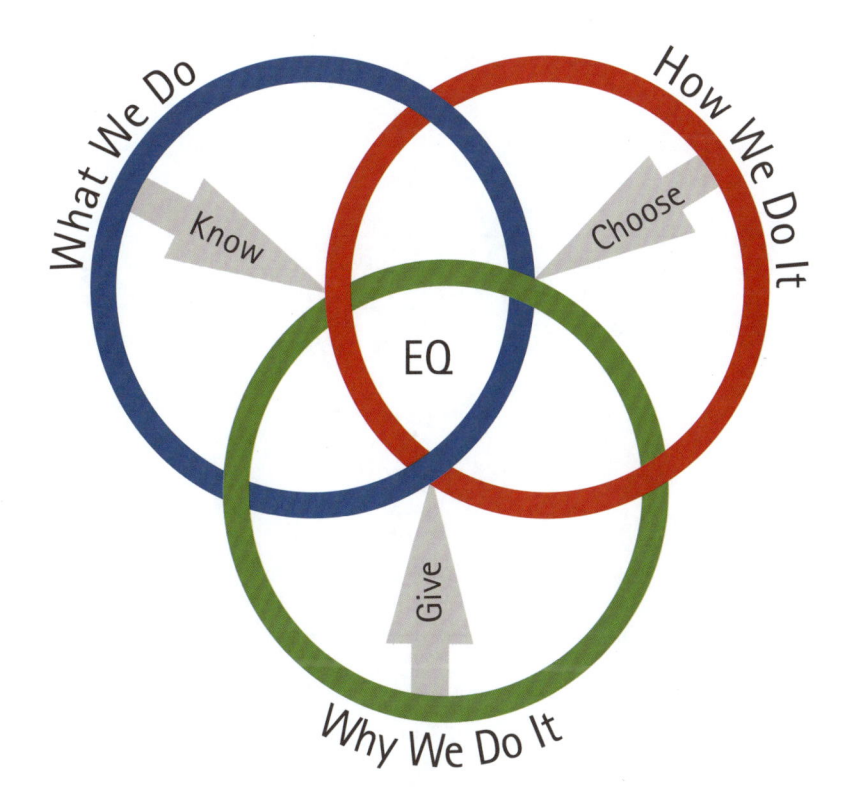

EMOTIONAL INTELLIGENCE

Exercise: Let's practice KCG. Complete the 123 KCG worksheet.

123 KCG

Situation:

Know Yourself

Tips: Use the Plutchik model. Listen to your body.
What am I feeling?

Choose Yourself

Tips: Pause. Look short and long term.
What options do I have?

Give Yourself

Tips: Remember your Noble Goal. What would you want? Check values and principles.
What do I truly want?

EMOTIONAL INTELLIGENCE

Exercise: Fill in the blanks using the word bank to complete the sentences.

1. EQ is so critical to success that it accounts for _____% of performance in all types of jobs (Bradberry & Greaves, 2009).

2. EQ accounts for nearly _____% of what moves people up the ladder and sets high performers apart from peers with similar technical skills and knowledge (Goleman, 2014).

3. EQ was positively related to _____ for both men and women, and at different levels of educational achievement (Sjöberg, 2001).

4. A strong link was found between _____ achievement and several dimensions of EQ (Goleman, 2014).

5. The World Economic Forum has identified EQ as one of the top _____ skills needed to thrive in 2020 (World Economic Forum, 2016).

6. Many recruiters are using behavioral-based questions addressing EQ in the _____ process (Lynn, 2008).

7. _____% of careers are ruined for reasons related to emotional competencies, including inability to handle interpersonal problems, unsatisfactory team leadership, or the inability to adapt to change (Bradberry & Greaves, 2009).

8. Organizations where EQ development is a priority are _____ times more times as likely to be high performers on the 4 Key Performance Indicators (KPIs) which are Retention, Productivity, Customer Focus, and Future Success. To put that in perspective: people who smoke cigarettes are 8 times as likely to get cancer (Freedman & Roitman, 2019).

9. Once you train your brain by repeatedly using new EQ strategies, EQ behaviors become _____ (Bariso, 2018).

Word Bank:

interview, 75, habits, salary, academic, 58, 10, 22, 90

Notes

POWERFUL QUESTIONS

What are Powerful Questions?

There are everyday questions and then there are powerful questions. Powerful questions stimulate deep thinking and promote positive inner growth. These questions open up the possibility to gain a wider understanding and a new perspective.

The skill of asking questions is more complex and challenging than many would assume, hence why using a taxonomy provides a helpful structure. A question taxonomy groups questions into different types and levels based on the difficulty of the expectation on the person answering. The L.I.F.T. taxonomy by Dr. Anabel L. Jensen and Cherilyn G. Leet is the first question taxonomy for social emotional development. The L.I.F.T. taxonomy stands for Literal, Interpretive, Fusion, and Transformative.

Below is a chart that further explains the L.I.F.T. taxonomy…

L.I.F.T.	Purpose	Example of Question
Literal	Uses data to gather a specific type of responses	What are your goals for taking this course?
Interpretative	Provides open-ended questions with multiple perspectives and responses	How are you currently using EQ to face daily challenges? How are you using them personally?
Fusion	Combines emotional data with discrete data; pass a judgment; your perspective or someone else's perspective with evidence	In your own life, what obstacles stand in the way of progress? What strategies have been successful to counter them?
Transformative	Provides an aha moment; challenges a cognitive bias; suggests a way to move forward with creative action; connects to lifelong purpose	In 5 years from now, what insights or skills would you like to demonstrate as a result of this course?

POWERFUL QUESTIONS

Why are powerful questions important?

Asking powerful questions is one of the most important EQ skills for personal growth and success. However, most of us have not been formally taught to craft or deliver powerful questions. The good news is that like EQ, it can be developed and improved overtime with practice.

Powerful questions can help us:

- Create aha moments
- Generate innovations
- Spark problem solving
- Reframe situations
- Encourage better decision making
- Discover our best self
- Clarify what's most important to us
- Sustain curiosity
- Foster joy and insight
- Intensify trust
- Build and strengthen relationships

The foundation of this course is based upon the use of powerful questions. As a learner, you will be asked to engage, respond, and generate questions of your own. We encourage you to look within yourself to find your own solutions to the questions. Your EQ journey starts now!

POWERFUL QUESTIONS

Throughout this course, we will be engaging in powerful questions to ignite your growth and development. Therefore, let's practice our ability to apply the L.I.F.T. taxonomy in order to develop and ask better questions.

Exercise:

1. Read the passage
2. Write a couple questions for each level of the L.I.F.T. taxonomy
3. Prepare to share

Injured, Alone and Afraid: Decision Making In the Wilderness
By Michael Miller, Six Seconds

"I took a tumble and sprained my ankle." "I'm sorry," I said, grimacing. There is hardly a worse place to sprain an ankle. And as I looked down, I could see Sarah's ankle had already started to swell. She couldn't put any pressure on it, and she had picked up a random stick to use as a trekking pole. As we hobbled down the path, we heard a sound coming from behind us. "Bear," I thought immediately, and I calmly yelled, "Hey bear!" to avoid a surprise encounter. But then the sound got closer, and it wasn't a bear, it was ... horses. And not only horses, but 7 horses and only 3 riders, probably a group coming back from dropping off supplies at a backcountry camp. It seemed too good to be true. The riders, with insignias on their shirts indicating a well-known dude ranch, stopped and chatted. Sarah asked if she could get a ride back down, clearly relieved. The guy who was in charge hesitated and seemed uncomfortable. "Look, we'd love to help," he stated, "but we can't. We're with an outfit and everyone who rides a horse with us needs to sign a liability waiver. And we don't have any on us. Sorry. Good luck." And they continued on their way.

POWERFUL QUESTIONS

Literal Questions:

_____

_____

_____

Interpretative Questions:

_____

_____

_____

Fusion Questions:

_____

_____

_____

Transformative Questions:

_____

_____

_____

Chapter One ———
KNOW yourself

Notes

CHECK-IN

What is check-in?

Check-in is a tool to help us learn to recognize emotions in ourselves and others. It offers the opportunity for us to develop strategies for navigating emotions. Check-in provides a "language" to talk about our feelings.

Why is check-in important?

How we are feeling on the inside can have a major impact on how we behave on the outside. Six Seconds reports that, "Emotions Drive People and People Drive Performance". If we aren't really aware of how we're feeling or how those feelings are influencing our actions, we are more likely to react versus intentionally respond in situations.

"Emotional awareness and understanding are not taught in school. We enter the workforce knowing how to read, write, and report on bodies of knowledge, but too often, we lack the skills to navigate our emotions in the heat of challenging problems we face" (Bradberry & Greaves, 2009).

Check-in provides the basic building block of EQ – emotional awareness. Practicing check-in is perhaps one of the most critical components to effective living. Overtime, check-in can become a powerful tool to develop emotional awareness and build upon our relationships.

CHECK-IN

One way to achieve greater self-awareness is to increase our emotional vocabulary. If we can accurately describe our emotions, the better we will be able to navigate them. Additionally, a large and robust emotional vocabulary opens the opportunity to communicate with others about our experiences and wellbeing.

Those without basic literacy skills tend to struggle with navigating big emotions and making authentic connections with others. The more specific our feeling word choice, the better insight we have into exactly how we are feeling, what caused it, and what we should do about it. Here are questions to ask yourself and others to gain greater awareness:

Know Yourself

Get data and consider:

- What am I feeling?
- Where are my feelings coming from?
- What is influencing or affecting my feelings?
- What am I thinking?
- What is influencing or affecting my thoughts?
- Where are my thoughts coming from?
- How am I reacting?

Choose Yourself

Pause and consider:

- What are ways in which I can choose a different thought or feeling?
- What are ways in which I can maintain the same thought or feeling?
- How are my reactions working – what are the costs and benefits of my current reaction?
- How else am I feeling?
- How can I gain energy and move this situation forward?
- How else can I respond – what are 3+ more options I have?

CHECK-IN

Give Yourself

Look forward and consider:

- What do the people involved truly want or need?
- Why might the people involved want to move forward in a new, more productive way? What do they need emotionally?
- What do I truly want or need?
- How might I step forward in a new way, more productive way?
- What can support me to practice EQ more effectively?

Notes

CHECK-IN

To enhance our ability to accurately identify and understand feelings, we will refer to Psychologist Robert Plutchik's Wheel of Emotions when participating in check-in and other classroom activities. There are eight basic emotions in the wheel: joy, trust, fear, surprise, sadness, anticipation, anger, and disgust.

Plutchik's Wheel of Emotions illustrates these eight basic emotions. It shows various ways they relate to one another, including which ones are opposite and which ones can easily turn into another one. This framework brings clarity to our emotions, which can sometime feel mysterious and overwhelming. To improve our understanding of emotions, Plutchik's Wheel of Emotions is a great place to start.

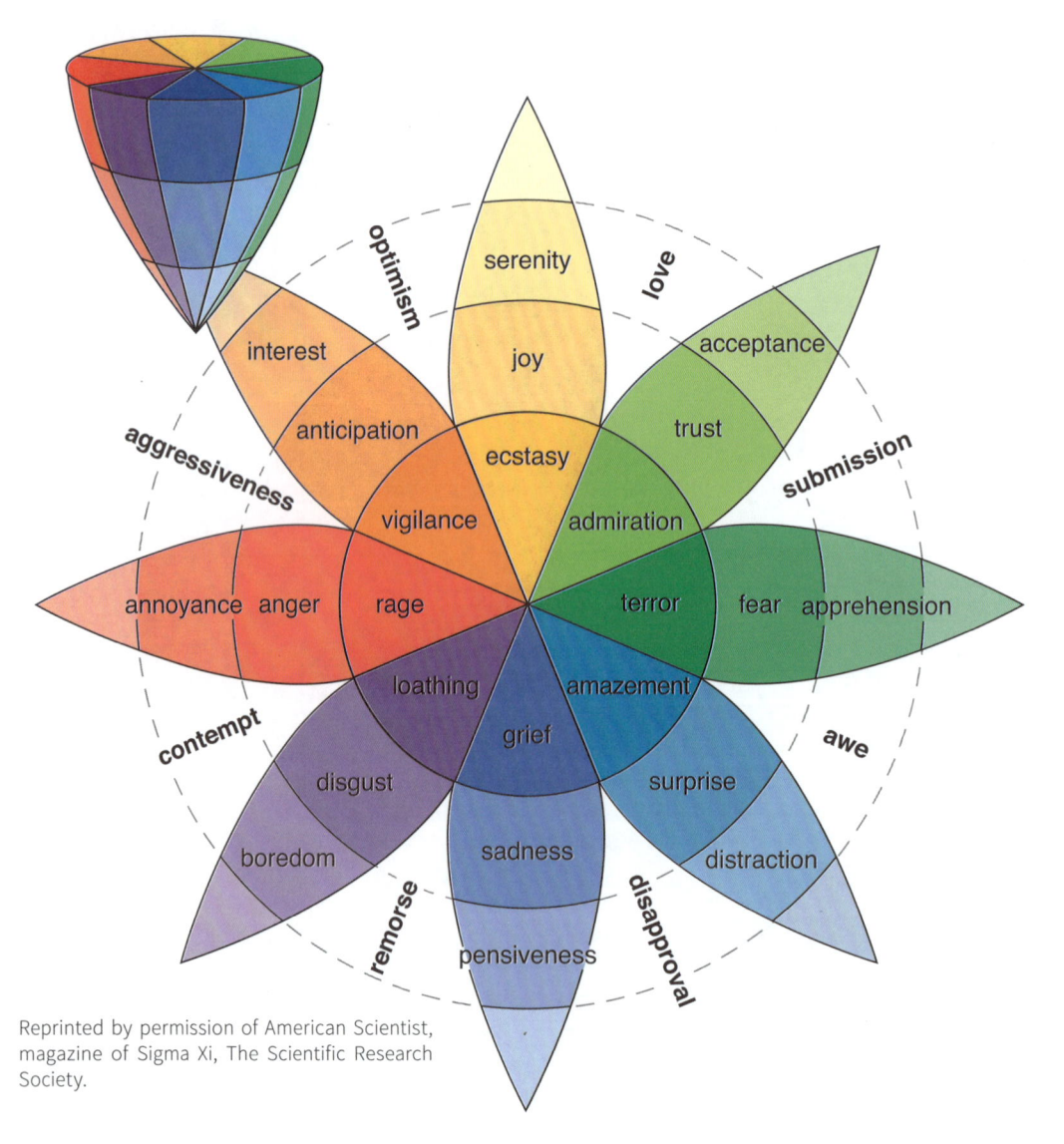

Reprinted by permission of American Scientist, magazine of Sigma Xi, The Scientific Research Society.

CHECK-IN

There are thousands of expressions for feelings in English, and the same in most languages. How many do you use regularly? Brene Brown's (2020) current emotional literacy research of surveying 15, 000 people found they can only identify on average three feelings in themselves and others.

What might happen if we had more precise and clearer words to understand our feelings and communicate with others? Below are additional useful feeling words to expand your emotional dictionary. If you don't already know all these words, use Google to find out. Then, consider: when do you feel them? How does each one feel? How do they serve you?

We encourage you to become a "self-scientist". Practicing "self-sciencers" believe it is significantly important to know who and what we are — and most importantly, what we are going to do about it. Science includes a process and method of discovery and investigation. Self-science is a scientific approach to the study of self. Becoming an "self-scientist" will help us discover, investigate, and understand our own feelings, as well as other people's feelings.

The EQ Feeling Chart, on the next page, can help expand our feeling vocabulary…

Notes

CHECK-IN

The EQ Feeling Chart

Afraid	Angry	Sad	Happy	Engaged	Moral	Belonging	Mixed
Insecure	Upset	Down	Peaceful	Absent	Nauseated	Mistrustful	Distracted
Timid	Disappointed	Blue	Content	Insignificant	Disgusted	Cautious	Sensitive
Shy	Prickly	Melancholy	Open	Stuck	Displeased	Lucky	Surprised
Startled	Frustrated	Bummed	Lighthearted	Dull	Provoked	Thankful	Dismayed
Concerned	Miffed	Gloomy	Confident	Numb	Shame	Trustful	Discombobulated
Frazzled	Peeved	Withdrawn	Pleased	Confused	Remorse	Caring	Playful
Unsettled	Annoyed	Lonely	Hopeful	Overwhelmed	Guilt	Connected	Cheeky
Uncertain	Irritated	Nostalgic	Optimistic	Distracted	Embarrassed	Loving	Goofy
Jumpy	Mad	Discouraged	Cheerful	Serene	Gratified	Welcoming	Wacky
Stressed	Critical	Deflated	Excited	Calm	Proud	Warm	Hilarious
Troubled	Vindictive	Weary	Eager	Focused	Self-reliant	Hospitable	Grateful
Anxious	Boiling	Disturbed	Joyful	Enthusiastic	Gratified	Accepted	Wahoo!
Worried	Fuming	Defeated	Delighted	Inspired	Fulfilled	Established	Amazed
Lost	Vexed	Heartbroken	Giddy	\multicolumn{4}{c}{Other feeling words:}
Frightened	Livid	Miserable	Blissful				
Panicky	Infuriated	Anguished	Thrilled				
Frantic	Outraged	Grief-stricken	Over-the-moon				
Horrified	Vengeful	Devastated	Exuberant				
Terrified	Furious	Distraught	Overjoyed				
Petrified	Explosive	Hopeless	Ecstatic				

CHECK-IN

The first layer of building our emotional vocabulary is to recognize, identify, and name our emotions. The second layer is more complex. Here we need to understand where our emotions are coming from, discover the root cause, and determine how pleasant or intense the feeling is. Adapted from *At the Heart of Leadership* by Joshua Freedman (2017), the Feeling Log (on the next page) will help us do just that.

Here's an example of how to use it...

> " I feel overwhelmed because I have been focused on a big problem. I would describe this feeling to fall under quadrant 1 with an intense, unpleasant feeling. I would rank my intensity as a 7.5 and my pleasantness as a 2.5. "

Notes

CHECK-IN

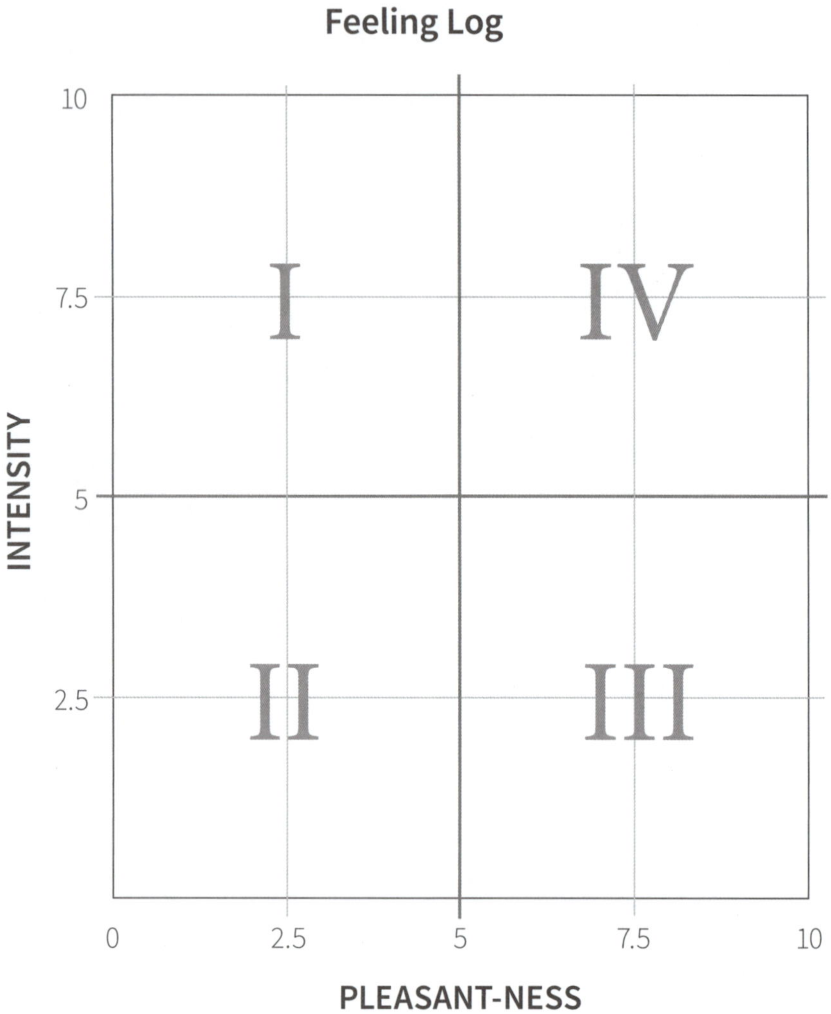

Feelings can be organized into these for quadrants; this helps provide a logical structure for understanding emotions.

- Quadrant 1 is intense, unpleasant feelings. Perhaps rage, grief, and disgust would go there.
- Quadrant 2 is mild, unpleasant feelings, such as boredom, irritation, or doubt.
- Quadrant 3 is for mild, pleasant feelings. Examples might be peacefulness, acceptance, or affection.
- Quadrant 4 contains intense, pleasant feelings. These might be ecstasy, adoration, triumph, or vigor.

THOUGHTS

WHAT ARE THOUGHTS?

Thoughts consist of our ideas, opinions, and beliefs about ourselves, others, and the world around us. Simply stated, it's our mind talking to us. Thoughts include the perspectives we bring to any situation or experience. Our thoughts can be productive, unproductive, or just plain neutral.

WHY ARE THOUGHTS IMPORTANT?

Canfield (1990) estimated that our brains have the ability to produce up to 50,000 thoughts on any given day. How many of your approximately 50,000 thoughts in a given day are intentional or conscious? It's different for everybody but it's essential to be aware of our thoughts and most importantly our unpleasant, unproductive, and demotivating thoughts.

Our minds are very powerful. A strong predictor of determining our destiny are the thoughts we feed ourselves. When we reflect on our own thoughts, we gain insight into how we feel and behave. This creates a space for us to re-choose and change our thoughts.

This single factor could mean the difference between success or failure. We have the power to choose.

THOUGHTS

Exercise: Identify and record the number of thoughts you have in a two-minute period. Follow the facilitator's lead to complete this exercise.

FEELINGS & EMOTIONS

What are Feelings & Emotions?

Emotions are reactions we have to things that happen around us and we use "feeling" words to describe them. There are eight amazing facts about emotions you should know:

- Emotions are data. Behind every emotion we feel, there is a signal delivering a message. If we ask ourselves, "What information is this particular emotion sending me?" we improve awareness.

- There are eight basic emotions. According to researcher Robert Plutchik's theory of emotions (1982) they are: joy, trust, fear, surprise, sadness, anticipation, anger, and disgust.

- Emotions are neutral. Emotions are not good or bad. Some emotions may seem more unpleasant than others, however all emotions serve an important purpose.

- Emotions come and go and can be mild, intense, or anywhere in between. Most of us feel various emotions throughout the day. Our emotions can last for seconds or longer which may turn into a mood. The intensity of an emotion depends on the person and the situation.

- We can try to ignore emotions, but it doesn't work (University of Texas at Austin, 2011). Emotions are a psycho-physical event, they work automatically and affect our body and our mind. Emotions are chemicals that exist even if we pretend they're not there. Emotions signal the body to prepare for opportunity and threat, regulating such basic functions as heart rate, blood flow, digestion, immunity, muscle response, and even body temperature. We can pretend emotions are not present, but the risk is to feel uncomfortable for long periods of time, and eventually, unfortunate effects on your health.

- Emotions are actually logical. While it's tempting to dismiss emotion as "random", every emotion has specific meaning. People behave in a way that makes sense given the emotions they're experiencing.

- Emotions are contagious (Iacoboni, 2009). A growing body of research has found that emotions spread from person to person through a variety of mechanisms, including a person's tone, voice inflection and non-verbal cues like body posture and facial expression. For example, an anxious boss creates an anxious office – just as a cheerful and smiling teacher can put the class in a good mood and create positive conditions for learning. Our

FEELINGS & EMOTIONS

emotions influence the response we get from others. Starting to take care of our emotional state is a good way to improve our relationships.

- Emotions are absorbed in the body in about six seconds (Pert, 2007). Emotions are electrochemical signals that flow through us in an unending cycle. It means if we are feeling something for longer than six seconds, we are – at some level – choosing to recreate and refuel those feelings.

WHY ARE FEELINGS & EMOTIONS IMPORTANT?

One of the most important aspects of being human is the fact that we have feelings — all day long. Emotions help us to make decisions, take action, avoid danger, and understand ourselves and others.

How many of us have received a comprehensive education on how to understand and navigate emotions in healthy ways? Often, we grow up with mixed messages about emotions such as – "Don't cry," "Be tough," or "It's not ok to express your feelings." No wonder it's challenging for us to understand and navigate our own emotions. It's important to recognize that we need to be able to understand our feelings and emotions before we can navigate them in healthy ways.

This course will provide you a comprehensive education on emotional development and growth. Put simply, it will give you the opportunity to become smarter with your feelings. Of course, it all depends on your motivation and willingness to work on YOU. We invite you to actively participate in the workbook, classroom discussion, and activities.

FEELINGS & EMOTIONS

THE WISDOM OF FEELINGS

Emotions serve to direct our attention and to motivate us – they are information and energy. Each emotion provides a signal of our perceptions of the world inside and outside, but these signals are not clear "signs", rather they are "felt" senses. Typically, we have a complex combination of emotions and thoughts and seeing through the layers is a challenge.

The next page shows a chart, adapted from Freedman (2020), that will provide hints to help decode the message. Select two or three emotions and fill in the boxes. In the next few days, complete the chart to explore the purpose of your different feelings.

Notes

FEELINGS & EMOTIONS

Emotion	Purpose/ Influence	A time I felt this…	Question to ask myself…	My feeling is telling me to…
Joy	Energizes us to flourish. Reminds us what matters most to us	eating	What did I want to repeat/ maintain?	eat move
Fear	Focuses our attention on the danger		What was at risk?	
Anger	Energizes us to attack, push through obstacles	crappy drivers	What was blocking my way?	calm down
Trust	Helps us to achieve goals and expand possibilities		What was I connected to?	
Sadness	Reminds us about who/what is important		What, that I love, was going away?	
Anticipation	Helps us look forward and beyond our current situation		What new (important) thing was coming?	
Disgust	Helps us maintain boundaries, principles, and values		What was being violated or rules broken?	
Surprise	Focuses our attention on something new, unexpected		What unexpected thing/event happened?	

STATE OF MIND

WHAT IS STATE OF MIND?

Our state of mind consists of what we are thinking and feeling at the current moment.

WHY IS STATE OF MIND IMPORTANT?

We have the ability to choose our state of mind through the choices we make. We can choose how we think, feel, and act. It's important to know that our state of mind is *temporary* and *changeable*. This means if we do not choose our state of mind, other factors, events, and even other people can control it. It is when we allow those "other things" to control our state of mind or "push our buttons" that we become powerless.

Dr. Ronald Siegel (2015), assistant clinical professor of psychology at Harvard Medical School, reported, "About 40% of what determines happiness is under our control. In contrast, only about 10% has to do with good and bad fortune. It's not mostly events, but our responses to events, that determines our level of well-being."

Let's think about it this way…

Choose Your State of Mind…Choose Your Response…Change Your Outcome…Change Your Life.

STATE OF MIND

For most people, it's easy to understand actions: they are visible (like throwing a ball) or audible (like saying hello), or at least physiological (like breathing).

Thoughts and feelings are often mixed together in our minds, which makes sense because they are literally mixed together in the way they're processed in the brain.

To distinguish, consider this:

Thoughts have an evaluative component: they are assessing data, and include assumptions about what's happening. For example, "he's not listening to me" is a thought – it's an assessment of the situation. Thoughts are mostly abstract; they are not something you can physically feel.

Feelings are experiential. You can literally feel them. "Ignored" is a feeling that might go with the thought above. It might feel like a slap in the face or a punch in the stomach, it's something you can viscerally experience.

Let's practice identifying each prompt as a thought, feeling, or action…

Nervous	Feeling
Yelling	Action
I can do this	Thought
Sad	
Hugging a friend	
Angry	
Relieved	
No one likes me	
I'm always going to feel this way	
Laughing	
Everyone's going to judge me	
I can try	

STATE OF MIND

I'm better than they are	
Guilty	
Taking a deep breath	
I can seek extra help	

Pick a current situation and in the boxes below briefly describe the situation and your associated thoughts, feelings, and actions toward it.

Current Situation	
Thoughts	
Feelings	
Actions	

STATE OF MIND

What can you choose?

Complete the activity below, adapted from Freedman & Roitman (2019).

Score each item by placing a check mark in the box, with 1 = no choice to 10 = total choice.

How much choice do you have about…

Item	1	2	3	4	5	6	7	8	9	10
Your Emotions										
Your Thoughts										
Your Actions										
Your Future										
Your Health										
Your Work Ethic										
Your Career										
Your Family										
Your Words										
Your Attitude										
Your Relationships										
The World										

STATE OF MIND

Answer the following questions…

1. In general, what limits our choices?

_____
_____
_____
_____

2. What increases and expands our choices?

_____
_____
_____
_____

3. How effectively are you using your power of choice? What would it look like if you expand your choices or choose more freely?

_____
_____
_____
_____

There is not a "right" answer to these questions. People have multiple emotions and the emotion-chemical process lasts for about six seconds (Pert, 2007). At some biological level, we are choosing our feelings. We learned that our feelings, thoughts, and actions are all interlinked. We may not have total choice, but Six Seconds believes that each of us always has SOME choice. The EQ challenge is to see that AND to choose effectively.

Notes

CORE VALUES

What are core values?

Core values are principles and standards that guide our decisions and actions. They are at the heart of what someone stands for. We all have our own personal set of values that were built from our life experiences. Our core values are often referred to as our personal guiding life goals.

Why are core values important?

When we start to develop our core values, we discover what's truly important to us. When we are clear on our core values, they provide a solid foundation especially when times get tough. They help us make important decisions and inspire us to live authentically.

At various points or stages of life, we might recognize that our core values do not align with our actions. However, when we make our core values fully present and aligned with our actions, life becomes more purposeful and intentional.

CORE VALUES

Exercise: Determine your values. From the list below, circle the values that resonate with you.

Accountability	Helping Others	Religion
Achievement	Honesty	Relationship
Adventure	Home	Responsibility
Balance	Improvement	Risk taking
Belonging	Independence	Safety
Bravery	Initiative	Security
Community	Joy	Self-discipline
Challenge	Justice	Service
Competence	Kindness	Spirituality
Connection	Leadership	Sportsmanship
Courage	Learning	Strength
Creativity	Love	Success
Curiosity	Loyalty	Teamwork
Discipline	Making a difference	Tradition
Diversity	Merit	Travel
Drive	Nature	Trust
Education	Nurturing	Understanding
Equality	Open-mindedness	Uniqueness
Excellence	Optimism	Unity
Exploration	Order	Usefulness
Faith	Patience	Variety
Family	Peace	Vitality
Friendship	Personal Growth	Vulnerability
Forgiveness	Power	Wealth
Fun	Pride	Wisdom
Giving	Professionalism	Work
Gratitude	Purpose	Create Your Own:
Growth	Recognition	
Happiness	Respect	

CORE VALUES

Exercise: Place your identified top three values and write them in the "Value" column in the chart below. Next, continue to fill in the charts.

	Value	What it means to me…	What it motivates me to do or not do…
1.			
2.			
3.			

	One action step to make these values more alive and active in my life…
1.	
2.	
3.	

Notes

CORE BELIEFS

What are core beliefs?

Our core values are fundamental to our core beliefs. Core beliefs are the very essence of how we see ourselves, other people, the world, and our future. They are deeply held core values that influence how we interpret our experiences.

A core belief is something we choose to believe – what we believe to be "right" or "wrong". Beliefs usually come from our experiences, events, environment, relationships, and are often from our childhood. The core beliefs that affect our lives are either empowering or limiting.

Examples of empowering beliefs:

- I'm loveable (people appreciate me)
- People are inspiring
- The world is full of opportunity

Example of limiting beliefs:

- I'm not lovable (nobody appreciates me)
- People are untrustworthy
- The world is dangerous/not safe

Why are core beliefs important?

Core beliefs operate as our GPS system; they navigate and determine our destiny in life. They control most of what we do each and every day. Many of our core beliefs operate at an unconscious level, so it's important to be aware of our personal belief systems (Dweck, 2008).

Empowering beliefs move us forward in life. However, limiting beliefs hold us back in life and generally lead to unfavorable outcomes.

When we choose to operate out of limiting beliefs, we end up with unproductive outcomes and strained relationships. Rather, if we operate out of empowering beliefs, we create productive outcomes and establish healthy relationships.

CORE BELIEFS

Exercise: Follow the facilitator's lead and answer the following questions.

> **I believe it is important to tell the truth.**
>
> **I believe everyone can be successful.**
>
> **I believe it's important to be #1 in everything I do.**
>
> **I believe family is more important than education.**

1. Which statements did everyone believe to be true?

2. What are some reasons why people could have different beliefs?

3. When is it acceptable for us to believe differently than other people? When is it unacceptable?

4. Fill in the blanks…

   I am _____.

   Life is _____.

   People are _____.

   Are these empowering or limiting beliefs? How do they impact you and other people?

5. Provide an example of when your belief(s) changed. Why do you think it changed? What impact did that make on you and other people?

CORE BELIEFS

Let's think of ourselves as an iceberg. Only 15% of the iceberg is above the water and can be readily seen. The rest of the iceberg (the other 85%) is below the water and cannot be seen. Our behaviors are a visual to others and the outside world – aspects above the water.

When we ask ourselves what's driving those behaviors, we get to see what's below the water. Our behavior is influenced by various aspects, such as our values, beliefs, and core needs.

In a sense, EQ lets us look under the water to see some of those drivers and to work with some of these underlying factors. In many societies of the world, there is exhaustive attention to the surface. To behavior. To clothes. To social media posts. But who we REALLY are is deeper.

What if we could learn to see ourselves and others, not just in a superficial way, but recognizing the profound, complex, and beautiful aspects of our humanity? Once we start to look below the surface, we can start to achieve that.

The EQ Iceberg

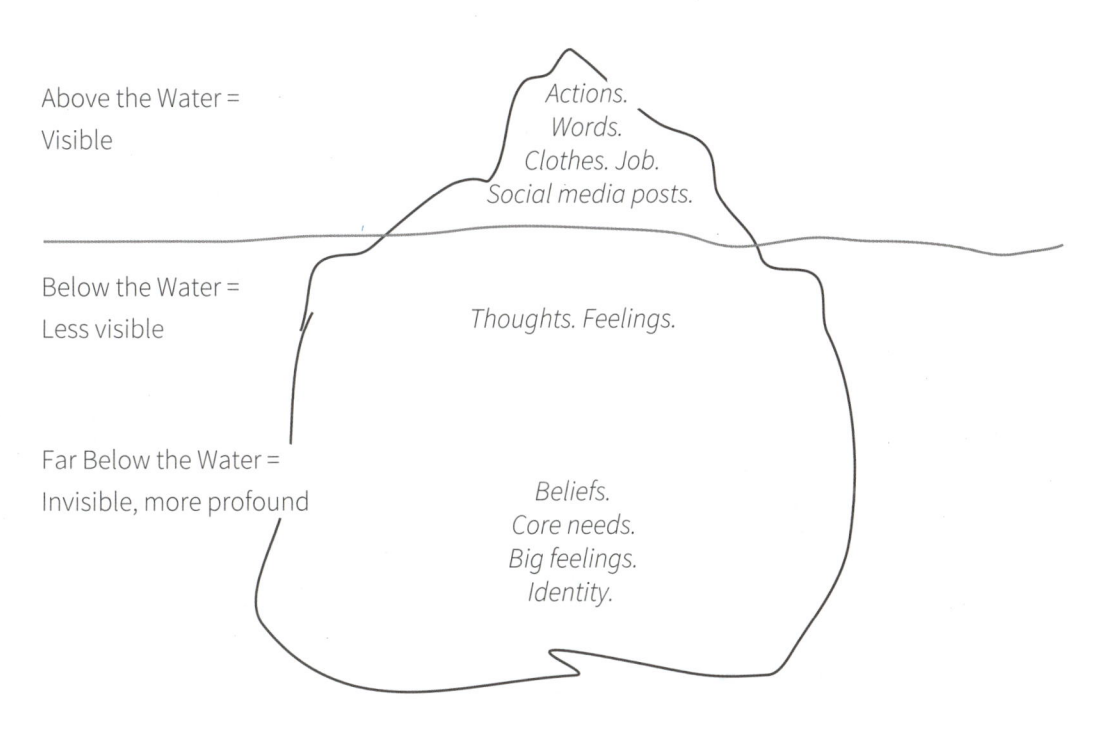

Above the Water = Visible

*Actions.
Words.
Clothes. Job.
Social media posts.*

Below the Water = Less visible

Thoughts. Feelings.

Far Below the Water = Invisible, more profound

*Beliefs.
Core needs.
Big feelings.
Identity.*

CORE BELIEFS

Exercise: Think back to a challenging event or situation you would like to get a deeper understanding of yourself. Create your own EQ Iceberg for that moment.

Challenging event or situation:

_____

_____

_____'s EQ Iceberg
(Name)

Above the Water =
Visible

Below the Water =
Less visible

Far Below the Water =
Invisible, more profound

SELF-CONFIDENCE

What is self-confidence?

Self-confidence indicates how good we feel about ourselves and how much we believe in our abilities. It's a judgment that we make about ourselves and reflects our ability to accept ourselves. Confidence comes from the Latin *fidere*, 'to trust.' Burton (2015) reports, "to be self-confident is to trust in oneself, and, in particular, in one's ability or aptitude to engage successfully or at least adequately with the world."

Why is self-confidence important?

"Scholars are coming to see (confidence) as an essential element of internal well-being and happiness, a necessity for a fulfilled life" (Shipman, 2014).

Self-confidence starts with truly believing in ourselves and our abilities. It takes practice and requires an accurate awareness of ourselves, in particular our strengths and weaknesses. Our self-confidence has a profound effect on how we think, feel, act, and most importantly the outcomes in our lives.

SELF-CONFIDENCE

When we play to our strengths, we tend to have more success. An analysis performed by Gallup, a global analytics and advice firm, revealed that people who use their strengths every day are three time more likely to report having an excellent quality of life. They feel happier, have healthy self-confidence, and are more likely to achieve set goals. Let's explore your strengths and new ways to use them…

Exercise: Circle your strengths from the choices below and/or add your own at the bottom.

Leader	Trustworthy	Determined
Creative	Loving	Appreciative
Helpful	Caring	Kind
Mentor	Patient	Problem Solver
Generous	Listener	Focused
Flexible	Responsible	Athletic
Disciplined	Humorous	Independent

SELF-CONFIDENCE

Exercise: Answer the following questions.

1. List the strengths you have that benefit you in your relationships (friends, family, professional, or romantic).

2. Describe a specific situation when your strengths helped you in a relationship (friends, family, professional, or romantic).

3. Describe one new way you could use your strengths (circled or listed on previous page) in your relationships.

4. List the strengths you have that help you achieve personal success.

5. Describe a specific situation when your strengths helped you achieve personal success.

6. Describe one new way you could use your strengths (circled or listed above) for personal success.

Notes

THINK, FEEL, & ACT (TFA)

What is Think, Feel, & Act (TFA)?

Our patterns include our thoughts, feelings, and actions and how they influence and interact with each other. Many believe there is a linear order between these three: they say thoughts come first, then we feel an emotion, which drives action.

Six Seconds highlights that current neuroscience shows something different: our emotions, thoughts and actions all influence each other.

An important step in Know Yourself is being able to notice how our emotions impact our thoughts and actions; actions impact our thoughts and emotions; and thoughts impact our emotions and actions. To be able to do so, we need to differentiate between these three.

Think, Feel, and Act (TFA) is a simple and powerful tool that helps bring our EQ into focus in order to see more clearly and act more intentionally.

The TFA tool has two uses, it is:

1. A model to recognize our thoughts, feelings, and actions in balance;
2. A process for re-choosing or reframing our thoughts, feelings, and actions.

Why is the Think, Feel, & Act (TFA) Tool Important?

It helps increase our awareness of our thoughts, feelings, and actions. The TFA tool provides a helpful way to recognize our patterns of thinking, feeling, and acting.

For example, imagine you have an upcoming job interview, and you think, "I mess up every job interview". Because of this thought, you start to panic. You become sick just thinking about going to the job interview. Because it is so uncomfortable, you decide not to show up.

The unproductive thought ("I mess up every job interview") led to an unpleasant feeling (panic), which resulted in an unproductive action (not showing up). What would happen if we changed this to a productive thought, feeling, and action instead?

THINK, FEEL, & ACT (TFA)

Event: upcoming job interview…

Thought: I'm going to mess up   *Re-choose*   **Thought:** I'm prepared

Feelings: Panic and stress   *Re-choose*   **Feelings:** Optimistic and hopeful

Action: I don't show up   *Re-choose*   **Action:** I show up confidently

We have a *choice* about our thoughts, feelings, and actions. EQ is about using and balancing all three. When we become more aware of these, we can *choose* to replace unproductive ones to productive ones. This simple and practical exercise using TFA opens up new possibilities that leads to productive outcomes in our lives and relationships.

Notes

THINK, FEEL, & ACT (TFA)

The TFA tool represents an important principle of EQ. There is a dynamic interaction of our feelings, thoughts, and actions. It is not a simple or linear process, but as we practice EQ we come to see these interactions more clearly, and expand our choices in all three areas.

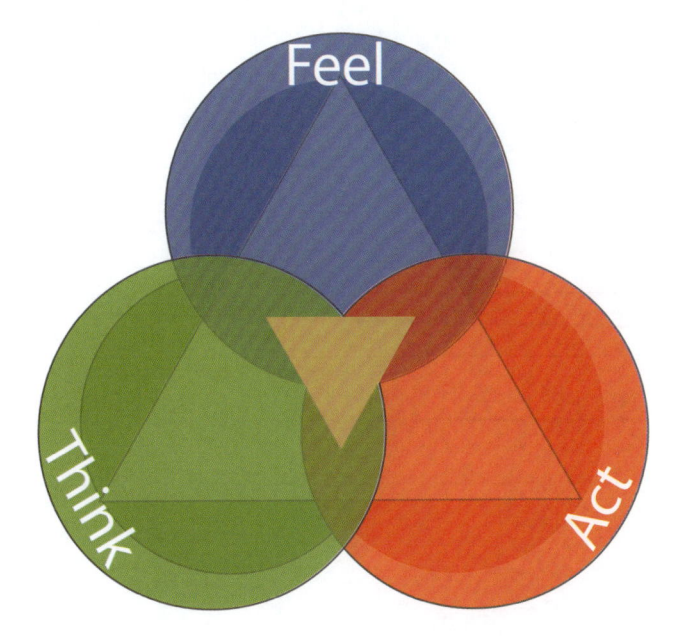

Let's use the TFA tool…

Step 1: THINK

Think of a recent situation (that didn't work out well). Think back half-way or 3/4 of the way through that situation: What were some of your thoughts, feelings, and actions?

_____
_____
_____
_____
_____
_____
_____

THINK, FEEL, & ACT (TFA)

Step 2: FEEL

If you were in a similar situation again, if you had the chance, might you choose any different responses? What feelings, actions, or thoughts might you prefer?

_____
_____
_____
_____
_____
_____

Step 3: ACT

Why might you choose that new response? What might be the purpose and human connection that fuels this change of actions, thoughts, and feelings?

_____
_____
_____
_____
_____
_____

THINK, FEEL, & ACT (TFA)

Keeping a record of our thoughts, feelings, and actions can help us see how they interact from our own experiences.

Exercise: Complete the following recording sheet for one week.

Event	My Thoughts	My Feelings	My Actions	Outcome

Notes

KNOW YOURSELF STRATEGIES

So far, we've discussed various EQ strategies to improve the EQ area of Know Yourself. Below are 10 EQ strategies designed to help us continue to grow and develop in this area. These strategies are based upon the concepts we have previously learned.

1. Acknowledge that emotions matter

2. Check-in with myself

3. Become a "self-scientist"

4. Write down my thoughts, feelings, and actions

5. Grow my emotional vocabulary

6. Recognize my state of mind is temporary and changeable

7. Explore my core values

8. Discover my core beliefs

9. Embrace my strengths

10. Use Think, Feel, and Act (TFA)

KNOW YOURSELF GOAL SETTING

Use the goal setting worksheet to help you achieve or further develop the EQ area of Know Yourself. To guide your actions, create your step-by-step plan below.

First, list three Know Yourself concepts (refer to *Course Learning Outcomes* section) that you want to achieve or further develop.

1.

2.

3.

Next, write down an action and deadline for each Know Yourself concept. For help, refer to the *Know Yourself Strategies* on the previous page.

1. Action: _____ Deadline: ___/___/___

2. Action: _____ Deadline: ___/___/___

3. Action: _____ Deadline: ___/___/___

Demonstrate one action step using the C.L.E.A.R. (Collaborate, Listen, Empathize, Adapt, and Reward) technique to boost your effectiveness to achieve your set goals.

What challenges might you encounter in trying to achieve your goals?

How might you overcome these challenges to achieve your goals?

Signed: _____   Date: _____

Witness: _____   Date: _____

Chapter Two
CHOOSE yourself

Notes

PESSIMISM

WHAT IS PESSIMISM?

Pessimism is characterized as one having a limited perspective of hope and possibility. Someone following a pessimistic pattern views problems as Permanent, Pervasive, and one that is Powerless. These are defined as…

Permanent: this situation will not pass and will last forever.

Pervasive: this is not an isolated event and it is affecting my entire life.

Powerless: I have no control of the situation.

WHY IS HAVING AN AWARENESS OF OUR PESSIMISTIC PATTERNS IMPORTANT?

This learned way of thinking and feeling causes us to become powerless, which leads to unwanted situations and unproductive outcomes. When we are pessimistic, we tend to get "stuck" in the problem and see things through a problem-focused lens.

In the words of Sir Winston Churchill, "A pessimist sees the difficulty in every opportunity; an optimist sees the opportunity in every difficulty."

A pessimistic outlook decreases our wellbeing, self-motivation, and the ability to hold productive relationships with others. This problem-focused state of mind leads to the inability for us to see beyond the present and take ownership of the future.

PESSIMISM

Exercise: Answer the following questions.

1. What does pessimistic mean to you?

2. How does pessimism show up in your life?

When you follow a pessimistic pattern...

3. What emotions do you experience?

4. What thoughts do you have?

5. What actions do you take?

OPTIMISM

What is optimism?

Optimism is characterized as one having a proactive perspective of hope and possibility. Someone using optimism views problems as Temporary, Isolated, and Effort is possible, also known as the T.I.E technique.

These are defined as…

Temporary: this situation will pass.

Isolated: this is an isolated event that is only one part of my life.

Effort: with effort, I can change parts of this situation.

Why is exercising optimism important?

Everyone uses both optimistic and pessimistic styles of thinking, some tend to use one more often. However, when we exercise optimism we see beyond the present and take ownership in our future decisions and outcomes.

Optimism can lead to a host of productive outcomes, including greater achievement, better physical and emotional health, and increased longevity (Rasmussen, Scheier, & Greenhouse, 2009). In areas ranging from performance in a cycling race to recovery after heart surgery, optimistic thinking has been shown to make a difference.

An optimistic outlook increases the pool of choices and the opportunity for success. This provides us a solution-focused approach, helps us innovate, and allows us to engage others' positive energy. Exercising optimism allows us to find opportunity, even in a challenge.

OPTIMISM

Exercise: To exercise the muscle of learned optimism, we'll use the T.I.E. technique in the following worksheet.

Super Pessimistic vs. Super Optimist

How can we find a realistic optimism?
Let's try this exercise…

Briefly describe a challenge or situation (for example: handling multiple projects at the same time).

Super Pessimist How would an EXTREME pessimist describe this situation?	**Super Optimistic** How would an EXTREME optimist describe this situation?

Realistic Optimist   What is a balanced but optimistic view of the situation?

What did you learn from considering these three views?

EMOTIONAL REGULATION

What is emotional regulation?

Emotional regulation describes our ability to regulate our own and other people's emotions. A variety of terms are used to describe this ability, such as, navigating emotions, managing emotions, and transforming emotions. Emotional regulation involves using EQ skills in order to increase, maintain, or decrease the intensity, duration, and/or quality of an emotion (Gyurak, Gross, & Etkin, 2011).

Why is emotional regulation important?

Regulating emotions, leads to intentional responses and decreases emotional reactivity in situations. Emotional regulation means that we decide and choose the content, nature, and intensity of our emotions.

For example, let's take someone who is feeling intense anger. If they are unable to regulate its intensity, they may display actions related to anger, such as fighting or displaying aggression.

Now let's consider someone who is feeling intense excitement. If they are unable to regulate its intensity, they may underestimate a risk and make a rash decision, such as taking out a loan to buy the newest piece of technology.

Remember just as an anxious boss creates an anxious office, a cheerful and smiling teacher can put the class in a good mood and create positive conditions for learning.

Emotional regulation skills help us learn how to navigate our feelings to better handle situations we are in. Strong emotional regulation skills can improve our long-term wellbeing and enhance our relationships.

EMOTIONAL REGULATION

A thermometer **reacts** to the temperature of the environment. Whereas, a thermostat **regulates** the temperature of the environment. People who operate like a thermometer allow external factors to control their emotions. On the other hand, people who operate like a thermostat determine the degree of their emotions.

When we practice Choose Yourself, we accept our emotions as they come and use them as a source of data. When we operate as a "thermostat" we can navigate, channel, and transform (not control or suppress) our emotions to purposely connect with others.

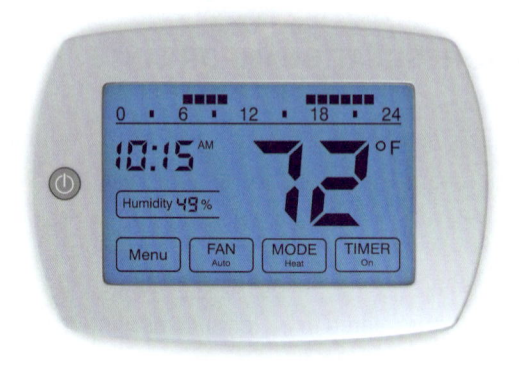

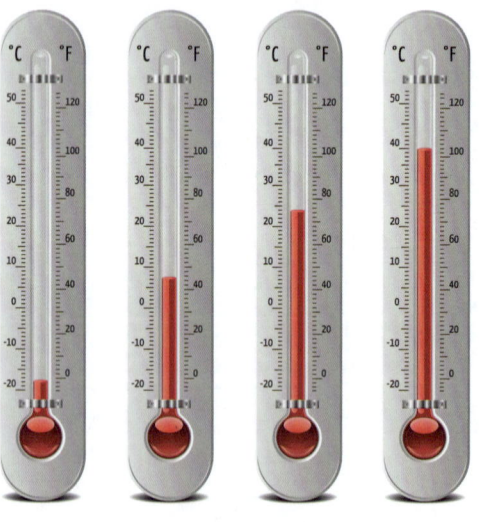

EMOTIONAL REGULATION

Exercise: Answer the following questions...

1. When am I a thermometer and when am I a thermostat? For example, I tend to be a thermometer at home and a thermostat in the classroom or at work.

   In other peoples problem - Thermostat

   My Problem - Thermometer

2. How important is it for me to regulate my pleasant and unpleasant emotions? Do I need to do this? Why?

   very, Yes bc Im mean

3. When do I turn up the intensity or degree of an emotion? How do I do this? Why should I do this?

   When Im upset, I just yell

4. When do I turn down the intensity or degree of an emotion? How do I do this? Why should I do this?

5. Describe a situation where you were able to regulate your emotions.

   When my parents yell @ me

6. Describe a situation where if you had been able to regulate your emotions, the outcome would have been productive instead of unproductive.

   When I yelled @ a girl in a parking lot

EMOTIONAL REGULATION

Emotion-chemicals last for about six seconds (Pert, 2007). So, any time we're feeling strong feelings for longer than six seconds, in some way, we're choosing to recreate the feeling. What if we pause?

Exercise: Follow the facilitator's lead in filling out the stop light.

- Breathe
- Recognize
- Reality Check
- Question Beliefs
- Empowering Beliefs
- Solution-Focused

ANGER

WHAT IS ANGER?

Anger is a normal emotion that we all experience from time to time. Anger is often called a secondary emotion (Denton, Johnson, & Burleson, 2009). We typically choose anger in order to protect ourselves from other vulnerable feelings. Anger often comes after feelings such as hurt, fear, or sadness.

WHY IS MANAGING OUR ANGER IMPORTANT?

Since anger is a secondary emotion, we have the power to manage our anger. For example, let's look at a relationship where anger arises quickly. The primary emotions they're experiencing might be afraid, lonely, and unworthy. These primary feelings may be influenced by the fear of abandonment and the thought of their loved one leaving them.

If we are unable to express and manage our anger in healthy ways, it may lead to significant problems at school, work, in our relationships, and in our health. The long-term physical effects of uncontrolled anger include increased anxiety, low self-confidence, high blood pressure, and lower quality relationships.

To promote healthy and rewarding relationships, the causes of our anger must be identified. When we realize how other emotions can influence anger, we can then use that information to our advantage by making healthier choices.

ANGER

Before we learn the techniques to manage our anger, we first need to learn how to recognize our anger. We need to determine how we react when faced with anger.

Exercise: Circle the warning signs that apply to you.

Draw a blank	Make an angry face *(circled)*	Become argumentative *(circled)*
Insult the other person *(circled)*	Raise your voice *(circled)*	Go quiet and "shut down"
Dizziness	Clench fists *(circled)*	Cry *(circled)*
Start sweating	Feel sick to your stomach	Pace around the room
Throw things	Shake or tremble	Headaches *(circled)*
Heavy or fast breathing	Feel hot *(circled)*	Can't stop thinking about the problem *(circled)*
Stare at the other person aggressively	Become aggressive	Clench teeth
Other:	Other:	Other:

ANGER

It may feel that anger just happens to us, but this is not exactly the case. Anger slowly builds and we must pay attention to it, but more specifically the feelings that come before it.

Exercise: Complete your anger thermometer. Consider a recent situation when you became angry. Think about the progression of your emotions.

Refer to Plutchik's Wheel of Emotions or The EQ Feeling Chart to help determine how you progressed from a state of calm to a state of anger.

Record your identified emotions on this scale, with 1 being a low intensity feeling (such as calm) to 100 being a high intensity feeling (such as rage).

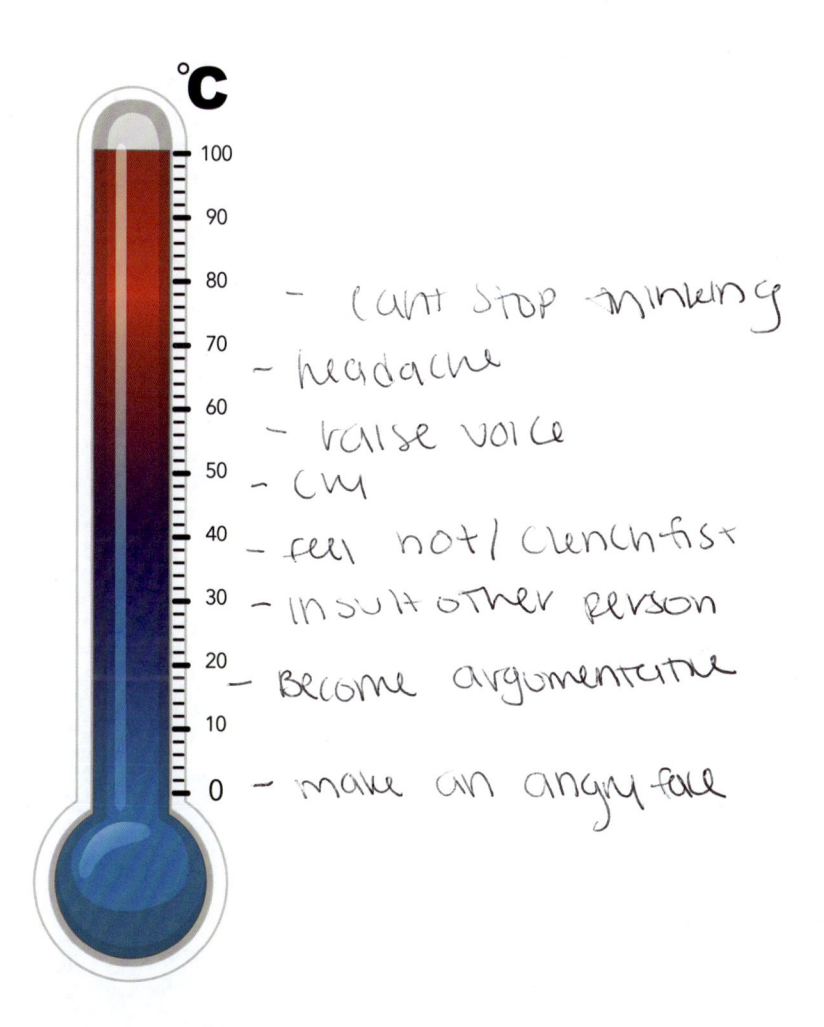

- can't stop thinking (70)
- headache (60)
- raise voice (50)
- cry (45)
- feel hot / clench fist (40)
- insult other person (30)
- become argumentative (20)
- make an angry face (0)

Notes

FEAR

What is Fear?

Fear is typically an automatic response to an uncomfortable or dangerous situation. Fear exists to protect us from a perceived threat. Fear includes a physical and emotional response to an event we are facing.

Why is Managing Our Fear Important?

Many of us experience fear. However, fear can be crippling if we let it. It can take away numerous life opportunities. Dr. Susan Jeffers (2007), who wrote *Feel the Fear and Do It Anyway*, states, "I believe fear is primarily an educational problem and that by reeducating the mind, you can accept fear as simply a fact of life rather than a barrier to success."

People often refer to fear as a "bad feeling" or even weakness. In fact, fear is a healthy and useful feeling for protection. It assists us to evaluate risks. Six Seconds states that one of the most powerful ways of using emotional intelligence is to consider all emotions are useful. When we experience big feelings, we should ask ourselves:

>What am I feeling?
>
>What options do I have?
>
>What do I truly want?

When we pause and check-in with ourselves, it can lead to making more optimal decisions. We can use fear to gain insight and re-educate our minds to face our fears and overcome them.

FEAR

Exercise: Answer the following questions.

1. What are some things that make you feel nervous or scared?

2. What do you think about when you are nervous or scared?

3. How does your body feel when you are nervous or scared? Circle the affected areas in your body…

4. What strategies can you use to manage your feelings of fear or nervousness?

FEAR

1

Fear is a question: What are you afraid of, and why? Just as the seed of health is in illness, because illness contains information, your fears are a treasure house of self-knowledge if you explores them.

-Marilyn Ferguson

2

May your choices reflect your hopes, not your fears.

-Nelson Mandela

3

Thinking will not overcome fear but action will.

-W. Clement Stone

4

We grow fearless by walking into our fears.

-Robin Sharma

5

F-E-A-R has two meanings: Forget Everything And Run or Face Everything and Rise. The choice is yours.

-Zig Ziglar

6

The thing about being brave is it doesn't come with the absence of fear and hurt. Bravery is the ability to look fear and hurt in the face and say move aside you are in the way.

– Melissa Tumino

Notes

POSITIVE SELF-TALK

What is positive self-talk?

Self-talk is our internal dialogue. It's messages we tell ourselves all day long. These messages can impact us. They can encourage and motivate us or discourage and limit us.

Positive self-talk consists of constructive thoughts that make us feel good about ourselves and our performance.

Some examples of positive self-talk are…

"I can and will accomplish anything I choose to do."

"I'm optimistic and hopeful."

"I accept the things that I can't change, and change the things I can."

Why is positive self-talk important?

Positive self-talk can improve our performance and happiness. A national study conducted on college students determined that students who practiced positive self-talk had higher rates of wellbeing (Neely, Schallert, Mohammed, Roberts, & Chen, 2009).

Positive self-talk can be a powerful tool for increasing our self-confidence and navigating unpleasant emotions. People who practice positive self-talk are more likely to be confident, motivated, and productive. We all have self-talk. Fortunately, we can learn to shape what that self-talk is. When we engage in positive self-talk, we begin to view ourselves in a more caring manner that increases opportunities of personal success.

POSITIVE SELF-TALK

We can't change the fact that we have been criticized and hurt at times or even that we have developed an internal critic. We can start to replace limiting beliefs about ourselves with empowering beliefs and affirmations.

Affirmations are positive (affirming) statements that one makes about oneself or one's actions. The best affirmations are **positive**, **present tense**, **short**, and **specific**.

Exercise: Determine and choose three different current events in your life and complete an affirmation for each event.

Event	Affirmation
Example: An important presentation	"I am a confident public speaker." "I am relaxed when speaking publicly." "I am excited when giving a speech."

POSITIVE SELF-TALK

When we repeat these positive statements over and over, they often:

- Become part of our subconscious mind
- Positively affect our state of mind and actions
- Lead to productive change in our habits

We can bring our affirmations to life by:

- Believing them as facts
- Saying them aloud
- Writing them down
- Posting them in visual places (bathroom mirror, planner, etc.)

How are you going to make your affirmations come to life?

....
....
....
....
....
....
....
....
....
....
....
....
....
....

POSITIVE SELF-TALK

Using words that are absolute, such as "must" or "always," can keep us locked into being problem-focused. We can change our thinking and our actions by avoiding absolute words and choosing solution-focused words that allow for change.

Exercise: Change the absolute statements to solution-focused statements by transforming the absolute words.

Absolute	Solution-Focused
"I can't"	
"It's never my fault"	
"If only"	
"My life is always a struggle"	
"Yes, but…"	
"I'm never satisfied"	

NEGATIVE SELF-TALK

What is negative self-talk?

Negative self-talk, also known as our inner critic, consists of damaging and unproductive thoughts that make us feel bad about ourselves and our performance.

Some examples of negative self-talk are…

"I'll never be able to do this."

"Nothing positive is going to come out of this situation. It just won't work."

"I am stuck where I'm at."

Why is eliminating negative self-talk important?

Negative self-talk hinders us from succeeding and allows us to make excuses for unacceptable actions. It can affect us in many damaging and limiting ways. One large scale study found that self-blame over undesirable events were linked to an increased risk of brain health problems (Kinderman, Schwannauer, Pontin, & Tai, 2013).

What we think and feel about ourselves comes through in our actions. Negative self-talk can become repetitive and it's possible to start believing it. If we believe it, then others start to believe it too. Learning to dispute our negative self-talk enables us to feel better and respond to situations in a more helpful and productive way.

NEGATIVE SELF-TALK

1

Your body hears everything that your mind says.

-Naomi Judd

2

Talk to yourself like you would to someone you love.

-Brene Brown

3

There is one grand lie – that we are limited. The only limits we have are the limits we believe.

-Wayne Dyer

4

You can and you will because you're badass like that.

-Jen Sincero

5

Your thoughts are your reality.

-Unknown

6

One small positive thought in the morning can change your whole day.

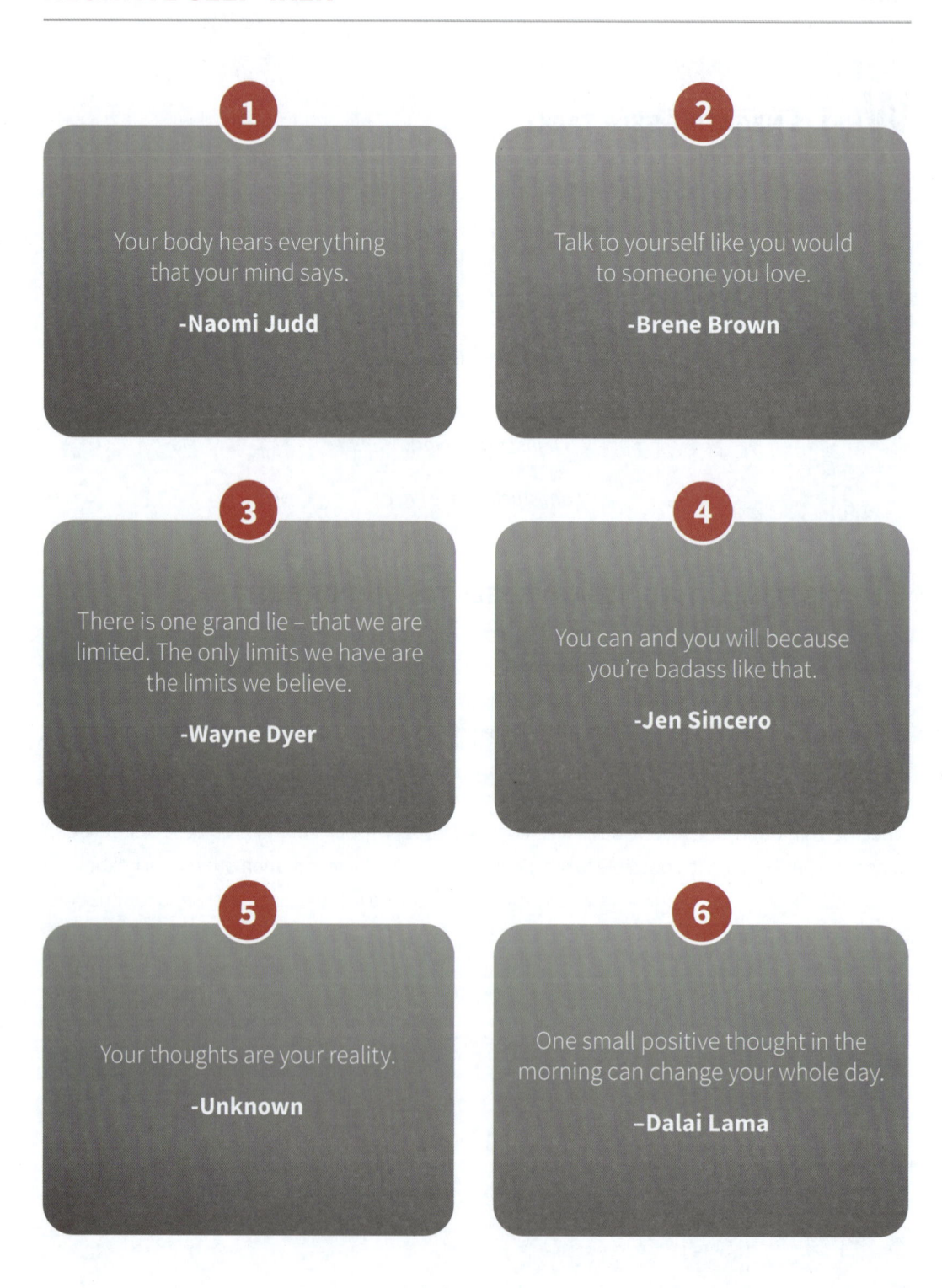

–Dalai Lama

NEGATIVE SELF-TALK

Exercise: Think of a recent personal or professional situation where you demonstrated both unproductive and productive actions. Next, complete the graph below.

Recent Unproductive Actions	What were your thoughts?	What were your feelings?
Personal or Professional:		

Recent Productive Actions	What were your thoughts?	What were your feelings?
Personal or Professional:		

NEGATIVE SELF-TALK

Answer the following questions…

1. What did you learn from considering both sides?

2. What were the factors that helped you to be at your best?

3. What were the factors that led you to be at your worst?

4. What did you notice about your thoughts, feelings, and actions? Did you notice any patterns?

5. Let's look at some of your typical patterns by inserting a thought, feeling, or an action in the blanks…

    a. When I think _____, I feel disrespected.
    b. When I make a mistake, I feel _____.
    c. When I think _____, I feel judged.
    d. When I think _____, I feel valued.
    e. When I think _____, I feel trusted.
    f. When I think someone isn't listening to me, I _____.
    g. When _____, I typically _____.

6. How might recognizing your patterns help you re-choose or reframe a thought, feeling, or action?

STRESS TOLERANCE

What is Stress Tolerance?

According to the American Psychological Association Dictionary, stress tolerance is the "capacity to withstand pressures and strains and the consequent ability to function effectively and with minimal anxiety under conditions of stress." It is the ability to identify a challenge as temporary and adapt to the challenge we face.

Why is Stress Tolerance Important?

Stress isn't always bad. Eustress is a type of stress that has been defined as a "good" stress. We need to experience this low-level stress in order to keep us healthy and happy. Low levels of stress make our bodies ready for everyday challenges by increasing our energy and improving our focus (Aschbacher, O'donovan, Wolkowitz, Dhabhar, Su, & Epel, 2013). Stress is a necessary motivator in our lives.

However, it becomes a severe problem when we experience extreme long-lasting stress. The quality of our lives is impacted by our ability to tolerate stress. According to the American Heart Association, unhealthy levels of stress are linked to numerous physical and emotional difficulties.

Stress can have an impact on our relationship with others. As stress increases, we become more task focused and reactive. Based on data from the American Psychology Association (2017), stress is up approximately 44% from the previous year—63% of people are stressed about the future of the nation, 62% are stressed about money, 61% are stressed about work, 57% are stressed about political climate, and 51% are stressed about violence and crime.

Our ability to effectively handle stress can lead to feeling less agitated, coping with situations more effectively, experiencing better health, and improving our relationships with others (McGonigal, 2016).

STRESS TOLERANCE

Exercise: Fill out the chart by identifying how you handle stress.

My Emotional State	My Physical State	My Actions
Example: Nervousness	Heart beats fast	Make careless mistakes

Answer the following questions…

1. How does stress affect you the most – emotionally, physically, or behaviorally? Explain.

2. In what ways can you reduce and/or better manage these responses?

STRESS TOLERANCE

Exercise: Pick one ongoing or daily stressor that you are experiencing and evaluate it.

Ongoing or Daily Stressor…
1. What was the last event related to this ongoing or daily stressor?
2. How did I think, feel, and act in this event? My thoughts: My feelings: My actions:
3. What are the consequences of this way of thinking, feeling, and acting?
4. How would you describe the consequences – either productive or unproductive. What was the impact?
5. If you determined your consequences were unproductive, re-choose or reframe your thoughts, feelings, and actions. Write your new empowering thoughts, feelings, and actions… My thoughts: My feelings: My actions:
6. What are possible outcomes/results of this new way of thinking, feeling, and behaving?

Notes

GRATITUDE

What is gratitude?

Gratitude is the act of being grateful and/or showing appreciation to others. The Latin root of the word gratitude is *grata* or *gratia* meaning a given gift. From this same root we get our word *grace*, which means a gift freely given that is unearned.

There are many ways we can express gratitude. Some examples include simple activities such as regularly journaling about what we are grateful for, writing a gratitude letter to someone, or performing a random act of kindness.

Why is gratitude important?

There is a wide range of benefits to practicing gratitude. Research suggests people who regularly reflect on what they are grateful for experience more positive emotions, feel more alive, sleep better, express more compassion and kindness, and even have stronger immune systems (Emmons, 2008).

Cultivating gratitude is an intentional practice that creates deep-rooted rewards. Gratitude allows us to strengthen our relationships, heal from difficult situations, and focus on the good in our lives even when times get tough. Given all the benefits of gratitude, it is imperative we practice these skills daily.

GRATITUDE

The simple activity of writing a gratitude letter can have powerful effects on our relationships. Below are steps to help you write a gratitude letter.

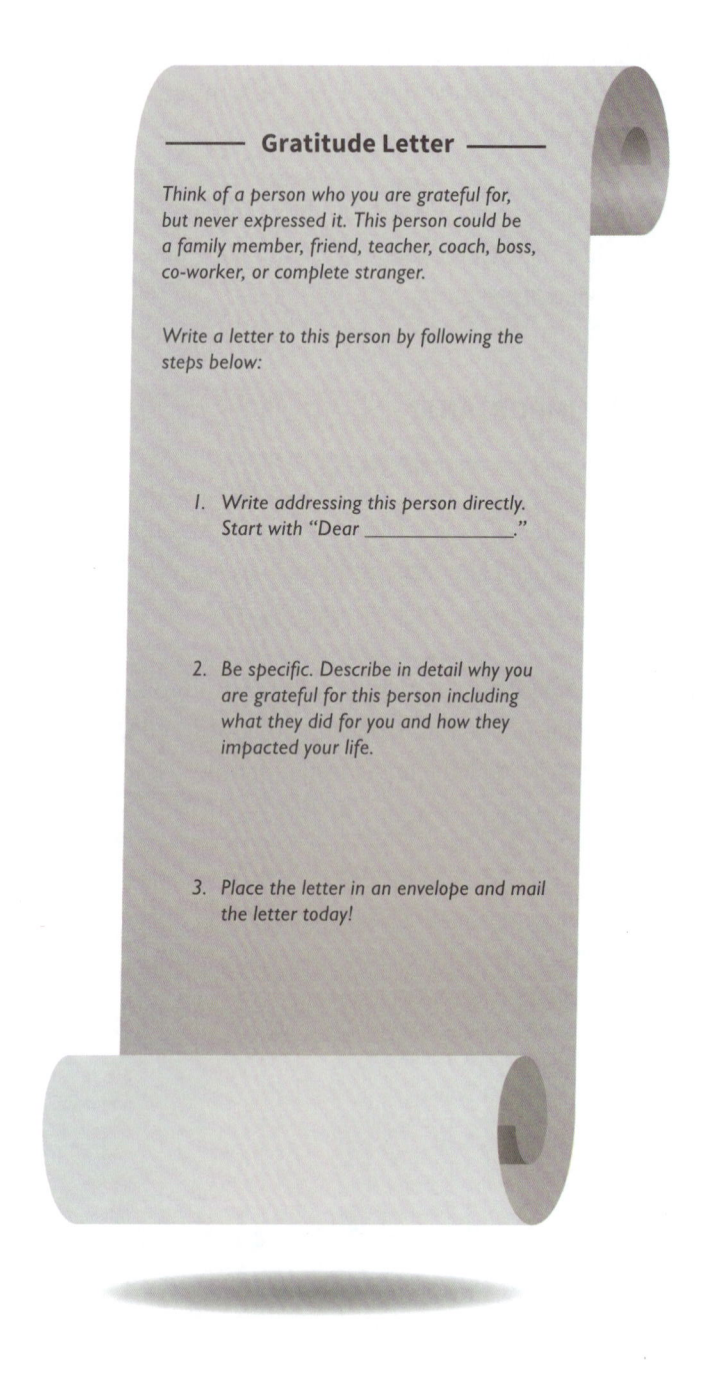

Gratitude Letter

Think of a person who you are grateful for, but never expressed it. This person could be a family member, friend, teacher, coach, boss, co-worker, or complete stranger.

Write a letter to this person by following the steps below:

1. Write addressing this person directly. Start with "Dear _____."

2. Be specific. Describe in detail why you are grateful for this person including what they did for you and how they impacted your life.

3. Place the letter in an envelope and mail the letter today!

GRATITUDE

Exercise: Complete your gratitude letter by following the steps on the previous page.

GRATITUDE

Exercise: Fill out a gratitude journal for one week. Use this template or a similar template of your own to complete your journal entries. See the back of the workbook for seven blank pages to complete your own journal entries – one for each day.

Date: _____/_____/_____

People I am grateful for today…
_____
_____
_____

One thing that happened to me today that I am grateful for…
_____
_____
_____

Obstacles that I was able to learn from today…
_____
_____
_____

Something I took for granted today that I am grateful for…
_____
_____
_____

Things I will do to make tomorrow awesome…
_____
_____
_____

GRIT

What is grit?

Grit is defined "as perseverance and passion toward long-term goals and describes sustained commitment toward completing a specific endeavor despite episodes of failure, setbacks, and adversity" (Duckworth, Peterson, Matthews, 2007).

Dr. Angela Duckworth (2016), the world's leading expert on grit, defines it as a combination of resilience, ambition, and self-control in the pursuit of personal goals that could take months, years, or even decades.

A number of factors make us gritty, among them are holding an optimistic mindset, a capacity to navigate strong emotions, and the ability to view failure as an opportunity for improvement.

Why is grit important?

Duckworth (2016) found that grit is the hallmark of high achievers in every domain. She also found that grit can be learned and developed.

Dealing with adversity is a continuous part of our lives. At some point, everyone deals with difficulties and hardships. Grit gives us the strength to move towards a solution in the midst of setbacks and challenges.

Being "gritty" gives us the ability to bounce back, and more importantly the ability to bounce forward. People who demonstrate grit are committed to overcome adversity, not just to survive, but to prosper.

GRIT

Exercise: Visit https://angeladuckworth.com/grit-scale/ to complete Angela Duckworth's Grit Scale. After taking the scale, answer the following questions.

1. What does grit mean to you?
2. Identify one person you know who is NOT "gritty." Describe how you know this person isn't very effective. What is their life like?
3. Identify someone you know who IS "gritty." What is this person like? What do you think made them this way?
4. Describe a time when you failed at something initially, but then with effort became more successful. What steps did you take to become successful? If you can't think of a time, picture something that you are struggling with now. What steps can you take to become successful? What EQ skills can you use?

GRIT

Exercise: Follow the facilitator's lead for this activity.

Let's practice exercising grit...

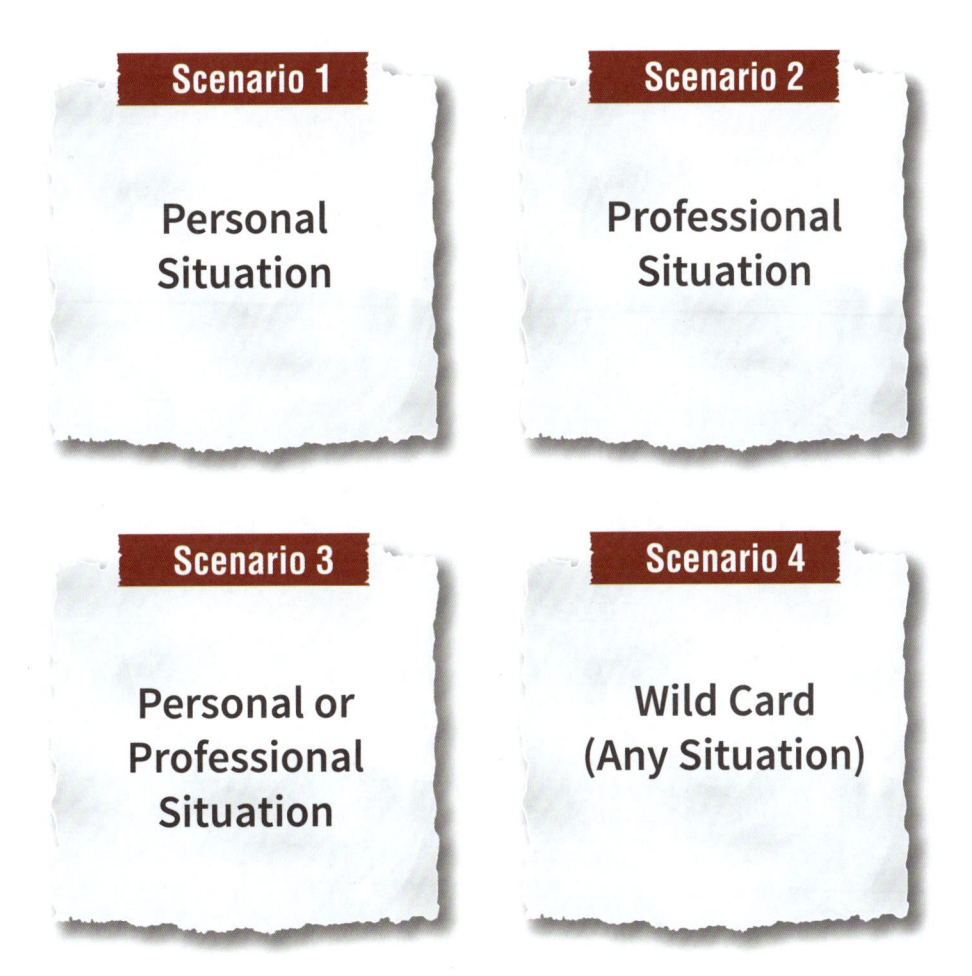

Scenario 1

Personal Situation

Scenario 2

Professional Situation

Scenario 3

Personal or Professional Situation

Scenario 4

Wild Card (Any Situation)

Notes

PROBLEM SOLVING WITH EQ

What is problem solving with EQ?

Problem solving with EQ is the ability to discover solutions to problems in situations where emotions are involved. A big part of problem solving involves understanding how emotions impact decision making.

Why is problem solving with EQ important?

Problem solving is valued highly in our economy. A new study found 62% of recruiters seek people who can find solutions (ICIMS, 2019).

A critical component of good decision making includes emotional awareness, more specifically the skill to identify, accept, and navigate emotions when faced with a problem. A person with high EQ views their emotions as helpful data in order to proactively work towards a solution. They respond to the problem in a healthy and effective way to help others and themselves. Whereas a person with low EQ fails to recognize their emotions and may react rashly to the problem in a way that exacerbates the issue.

When presented with a problem or a difficult situation, successful people find it in their power to discover solutions. They use their emotions to effectively solve problems and make optimal choices.

PROBLEM SOLVING WITH EQ

Before we jump into a problem, it's important for us to take a pause. We need to ask ourselves questions before trying to solve a problem. This will help us move away from automatic reactions and lead us to create intentional responses when faced with a problem.

Exercise: Think of a current problem you are facing. Keeping your problem in mind, answer the following questions in each KCG section.

STEPS	Questions to ask myself when faced with a problem
Know Yourself	What am I feeling? How am I reacting?
Choose Yourself	What choices do I have? What are the implications?
Give Yourself	What do I really want? How do I support and engage others?

PROBLEM SOLVING WITH EQ

Exercise: Read the scenario and answer the following questions.

Kelly and her partner agreed on how they would share daily chores for their home. They agreed that Kelly would be responsible for wiping down the counters and sweeping the floors and her partner would clean and put away the dishes. Kelly's partner consistently neglected to do the agreed chores and would constantly make excuses for not being able to complete them.

1. If you were Kelly, what thoughts and feelings would you likely experience?

2. How would those thoughts and feelings influence your problem solving abilities?

3. "The dishes are not done" is not the root of the problem. What is the root problem?

4. What would your thoughts and feelings be now that you have identified the root problem?

5. How could you use KCG to approach the problem?

6. How might you contribute to a solution in this situation?

Notes

CONSEQUENTIAL THINKING

What is consequential thinking?

Consequential thinking is a strategy that allows us to create productive outcomes by assessing the effects of our actions before making a choice. It involves taking a pause, or a moment, to view the situation and potential outcomes before acting. This strategy allows us to determine what might be best for us and for others involved.

Six Seconds explains three steps to apply consequential thinking, they are…

1. **Pause.** The first step is to pause. For how long? Just six seconds makes a huge difference. Emotions come from the arousal of the nervous system. Millions of chemical reactions take place as a result. The four most important are serotonin, endorphins, oxytocin, and dopamine. It takes the body about six seconds for these molecules of emotion to get absorbed back in your body after they are produced. So, give yourself six seconds and go from there!

2. **Evaluate.** This pause also offers an opportunity to evaluate the situation at hand. It may help to ask yourself questions about your short-term and long-term goals. What do I want to get accomplished? Is my current course of action helping me to accomplish those goals?

3. **Respond.** Now that you have paused and evaluated the situation, you are ready to respond more effectively.

Why is consequential thinking important?

Imagine that when we make a mistake, we could have the ability to pause, rewind, and do it over. Since that is not the case, we need to learn to pause BEFORE we take action and evaluate the consequences before making a decision.

Consequential thinking gives us control over our state of mind and allows us to navigate strong emotions effectively. Instead of letting strong emotions hijack our rational thinking, we can take a pause to consider the consequences of our actions and weigh alternatives.

Research from Ohio St. University found that people tend to make better decisions when they weigh the pros and cons of at least three options (Smith & Krajbich, 2018). Applying consequential thinking gives us the opportunity to pause, evaluate and respond, rather than react on autopilot. In turn we can make better choices and live more meaningful lives.

CONSEQUENTIAL THINKING

Exercise: Refer to the consequential thinking formula and answer the following questions.

Choices ⟶ Consequences ⟶ Helps me/us
                      ⟶ Hurts me/us

Ask yourself these questions:

If I make a choice and do _____, what might happen?

Instead of doing _____, what other actions can I identify?

Which of these choices will generate the most positive outcome?

What will happen if I do nothing?

1. Describe a situation in which you used consequential thinking.

2. Describe a situation in which using consequential thinking could have made a difference.

3. What might be challenging in using consequential thinking?

4. How can you overcome those particular challenges?

CONSEQUENTIAL THINKING

Exercise: The example below shows how to apply the consequential thinking formula. After reviewing reaction #1, #2, and #3, fill in possible short-term and long-term consequences for reaction #4 and #5.

Scenario: At the grocery store checkout line and the person in front of me is taking a long time.

Reaction #1: I may decide to tell the person in a rude tone to hurry up.

Short-term: Inability to resolve the issue
Long-term: Continued undesirable feelings and behaviors towards others in future conflict situations

Reaction #2: I may make a rude comment (underneath my breath).

Short-term: Inability to resolve the issue
Long-term: Continued undesirable feelings and behaviors towards others in future conflict situations

Reaction #3: I understand this person is not intentionally trying to go slow.

Short-term: Moving towards acceptance in order to help resolve the issue
Long-term: Increased ability to practice understanding towards others in various future situations

Reaction #4: I can move to another line.

Short-term:

Long-term:

Reaction #5: I engage in self-reflection and ask myself, "Why did I not leave myself enough time?" and "What should I do next time to plan around this pattern?"

Short-term:

Long-term:

CONSEQUENTIAL THINKING

Answer the following questions…

1. Describe a similar situation you have experienced.

2. How did you respond?

3. What do you think was driving your response?

4. If you thought your response was appropriate, what EQ skills did you utilize to help you?

5. If you thought your response was inappropriate, what EQ skills could you have used to help you?

6. How do you see yourself using consequential thinking in your future interactions, relationships and decision-making efforts?

RESPONSIBILITY TAKING

What is responsibility taking?

Responsibility taking is recognizing that we are responsible for our own happiness. It is not blaming others for our unhappiness. Responsibility taking is actively focusing on the things we can control…our thoughts…our feelings…and our actions.

Why is responsibility taking important?

A core component of Dr. Martin Seligman's (2006) theory of learned optimism, which has been found to reduce levels of anxiety and depression, is realizing that your effort will make a difference in the eventual outcome. Responsibility is POWER. Taking responsibility of our thoughts, feelings, and actions allows us the opportunity to choose how we respond to life's challenges. It empowers us to create our own happiness.

Viktor Frankl, a Holocaust survivor, devoted his life to studying, understanding, and encouraging "meaning." Frankl believed having a meaningful life begins with taking responsibility. He wrote, "Everything can be taken from a man but one thing: the last of the human freedoms— to choose one's attitude in any given set of circumstances, to choose one's own way."

If we don't take responsibility for ourselves, we may resort to blaming others which locks us into the problem. This makes us a powerless victim. Accepting responsibility provides us freedom and the ability to take action.

RESPONSIBILITY TAKING

Exercise: Rank yourself on how well you take responsibility for each statement, with 1 as "blaming others (or external factors) for my decisions and actions" to 10 "taking responsibility for my actions and decisions."

1	2	3	4	5	6	7	8	9	10
blaming			½ responsible				taking responsibility		

1. _____ I am responsible for the level of consciousness (attention) I bring to my activities.

2. _____ I am responsible for my thoughts and feelings.

3. _____ I am responsible for my actions.

4. _____ I am responsible for my beliefs.

5. _____ I am responsible for my values by which I live.

6. _____ I am responsible for how I prioritize my time.

7. _____ I am responsible for how I deal with people.

8. _____ I am responsible for my own happiness.

9. _____ I am responsible for my life and wellbeing.

Answer the following questions…

1. In general, what holds you back from taking responsibility?

_____
_____
_____

2. What motivates you to take responsibility?

_____
_____
_____

RESPONSIBILITY TAKING

3. How effectively are you using your power of choice when it comes to responsibility? What would it look like if you expand your choices or choose more freely?

___

___

___

Again, there is not a "right" answer to these questions. We may not have total choice, but Six Seconds believes that each of us always has SOME choice. The EQ challenge is to see that, AND to choose effectively.

Notes

RESPONSIBILITY TAKING

Exercise: Answer the following questions.

1. What does it mean to take responsibility for your own actions? What difference does this make?

2. Describe a situation where taking responsibility could have made a difference.

3. In what areas in your life are you taking responsibility (home, work, school, friend, society)? Be specific.

4. In what areas in your life are you not taking responsibility (home, work, school, friend, society)? Be specific. What changes can you make to start taking responsibility?

IMPULSE CONTROL

What is impulse control?

Impulse control, also known as delayed gratification, is the ability to resist or delay a temptation to act. It is not acting upon short-term gratification but working towards long-term goals and future outcomes. Impulse control can be looked at as *putting on the brakes* to something or someone.

Why is impulse control important?

We live in a fast-paced society that demands immediate feedback and gratification, and the challenge to think before acting becomes clearly difficult. We experience life and relationships in a world mainly focused of red and green…stop and go…with little or no time for yellow, the *putting on the brakes*.

Putting on the brakes often prevents negative consequences that come with a lack of impulse control. Our inability to pause before acting can lead to many damaging problems for us and our relationships. Acting on impulses exists in the reacting category of our lives. When we simply react impulsively, an action is taken without necessarily thinking about a future outcome.

Managing our impulses leads to outcomes that are more intentional, purposeful, and focused towards long-term planning (Cobb-Clark, Dahmann, Kamhöfer, Schildberg-Hörisch, 2019). Impulse control is a critical skill that prevents us from doing things that we probably should not do.

IMPULSE CONTROL

Exercise: Answer the following questions.

1. Describe one of the most impulsive actions you have taken.

2. What were the short-term consequences of this action?

3. What were the long-term consequences of this action?

4. What could you have changed that would have made you avoid acting upon the impulse?

5. What are some strategies you could use or are using to improve impulse control?

6. Are there times you are overly controlling your impulses? When should you be more spontaneous?

IMPULSE CONTROL

Exercise: Follow the facilitator's lead for this activity.

Let's practice impulse control…

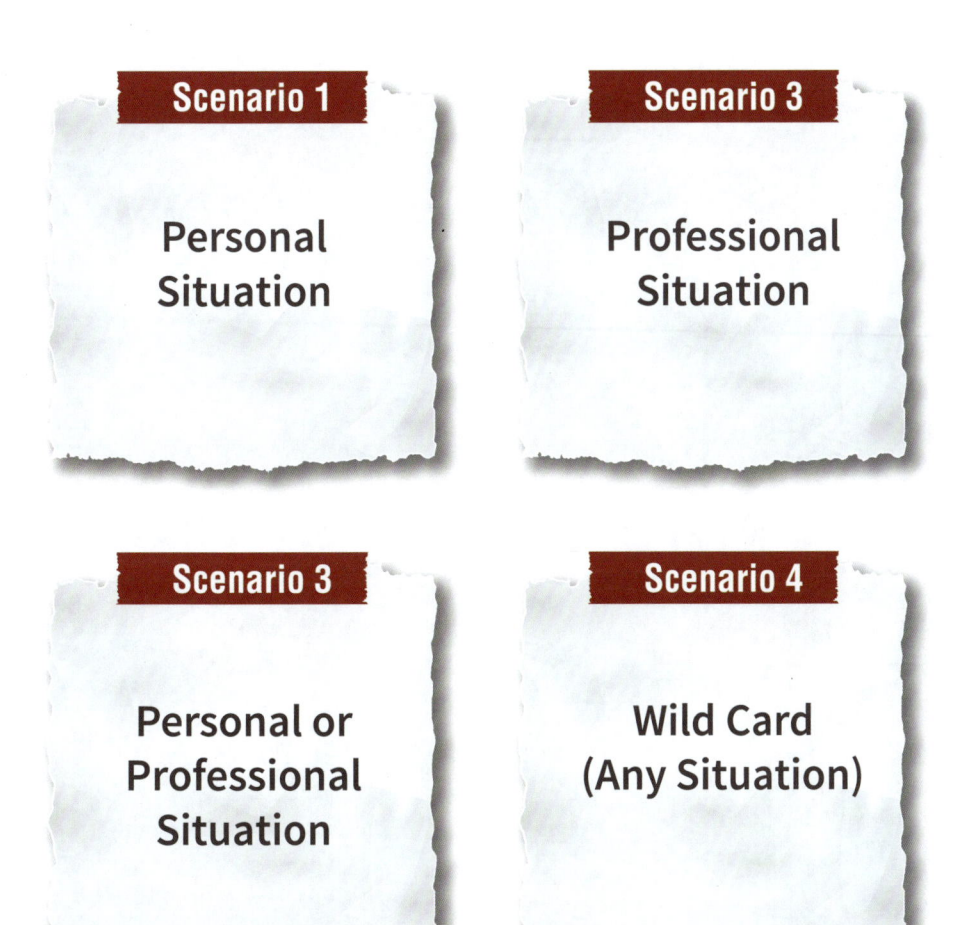

Scenario 1
Personal Situation

Scenario 3
Professional Situation

Scenario 3
Personal or Professional Situation

Scenario 4
Wild Card (Any Situation)

Notes

POSITIVE SELF-INTEREST (PSI)

What is Positive Self-Interest (PSI)?

Another way to think about positive self-interest (PSI) is self-care.

Webster's dictionary defines self-care as "the practice of taking an active role in protecting one's own wellbeing and happiness, in particular during periods of stress."

PSI is honoring our needs and wants in order to fulfill our potential and purpose. Selfish, on the other hand, is choosing to *only* think of our own needs and wants. PSI describes the actions taken in order to reach our optimal health and wellbeing in order to serve others better.

Self-care activities are personal and individualized. They look different for everyone. Some examples are journaling, saying words of affirmations, asking for help, watching your favorite movie, or sticking to a healthy nutrition plan.

Why is Positive Self-Interest Important?

When we attempt to meet the needs of family members, friends, employers, or society in general before meeting our own needs this can take a dramatic toll on us physically and emotionally. We are more giving of our fullest selves, when we take responsibility to ensure our needs are met.

Research performed by Kaufman & Jauk (2020) reported that high levels of PSI, defined as healthy selfishness in their study, can have a positive impact on the well-being of one's own self as well as the well-being of others.

There are many benefits of practicing self-care including better productivity, improved resistance to disease, better physical health, enhanced self-confidence, and enriched relationships. With self-care, we develop a good relationship with ourselves and therefore with others without sacrificing our health, our wellbeing, and our worth.

POSITIVE SELF-INTEREST (PSI)

Exercise: Review the *Circle of Intention* wheel. On the next page, create your own *Circle of Intention* wheel by identifying your wellness areas (outer edge of the circle) and self-care action steps (pie pieces of the circle).

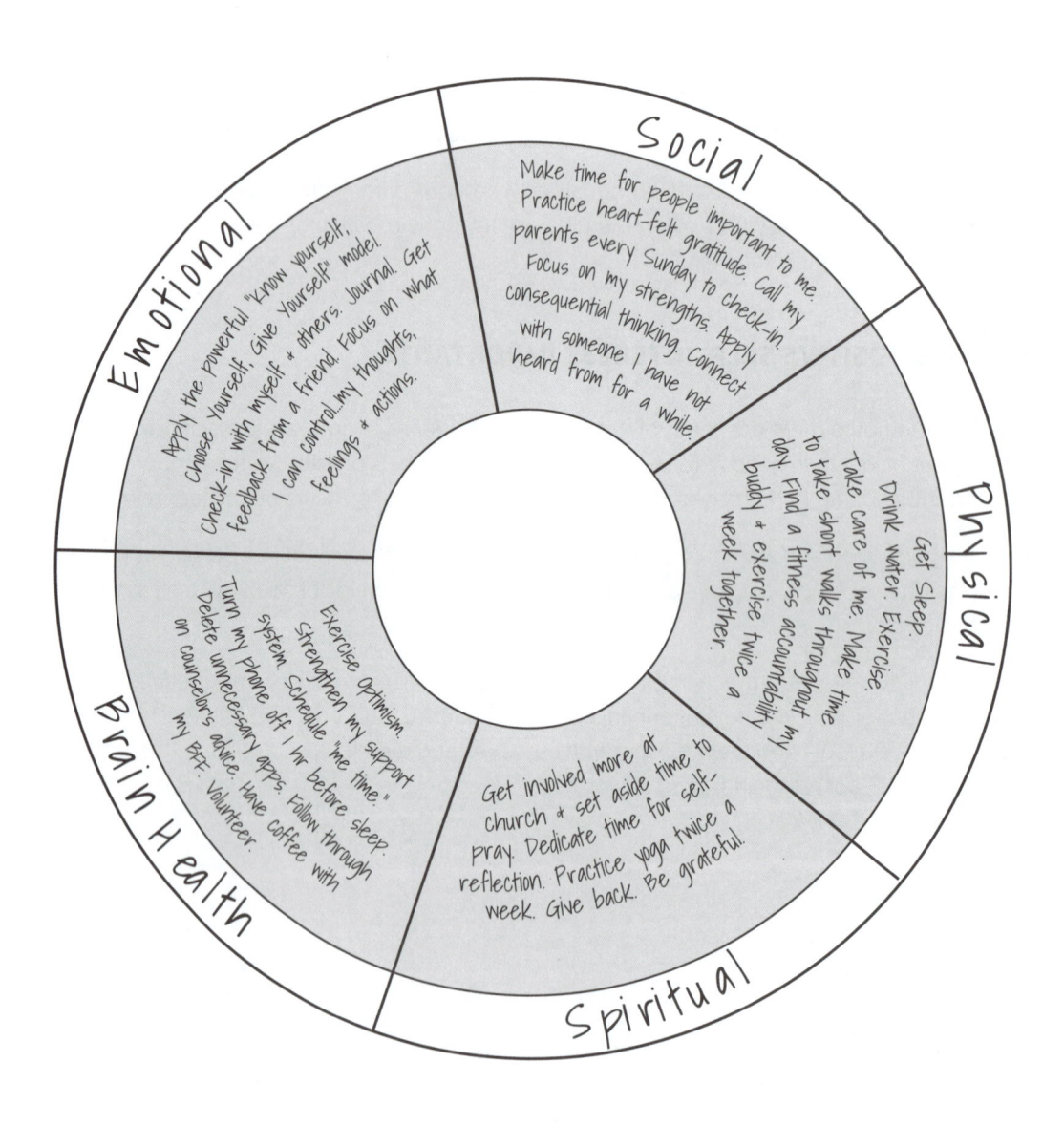

Social: Make time for people important to me. Practice heart-felt gratitude. Call my parents every Sunday to check-in. Focus on my strengths. Apply consequential thinking. Connect with someone I have not heard from for a while.

Emotional: Apply the powerful "Know Yourself, Choose Yourself, Give Yourself" model. Check-in with myself & others. Journal. Get feedback from a friend. Focus on what I can control. My thoughts, feelings & actions.

Physical: Get sleep. Drink water. Exercise. Take care of me. Make time to take short walks throughout my day. Find a fitness accountability buddy & exercise twice a week together.

Brain Health: Exercise Optimism. Strengthen my support system. Schedule "me time." Turn my phone off 1 hr before sleep. Delete unnecessary apps. Follow through on counselor's advice. Have coffee with my BFF. Volunteer.

Spiritual: Get involved more at church & set aside time to pray. Dedicate time for self-reflection. Practice yoga twice a week. Give back. Be grateful.

POSITIVE SELF-INTEREST (PSI)

Exercise: Create your own *Circle of Intention* wheel by identifying your wellness areas (outer edge of circle) and self-care action steps (pie pieces of circle). Indicate at least three self-care action steps for each wellness area.

Circle of Intention

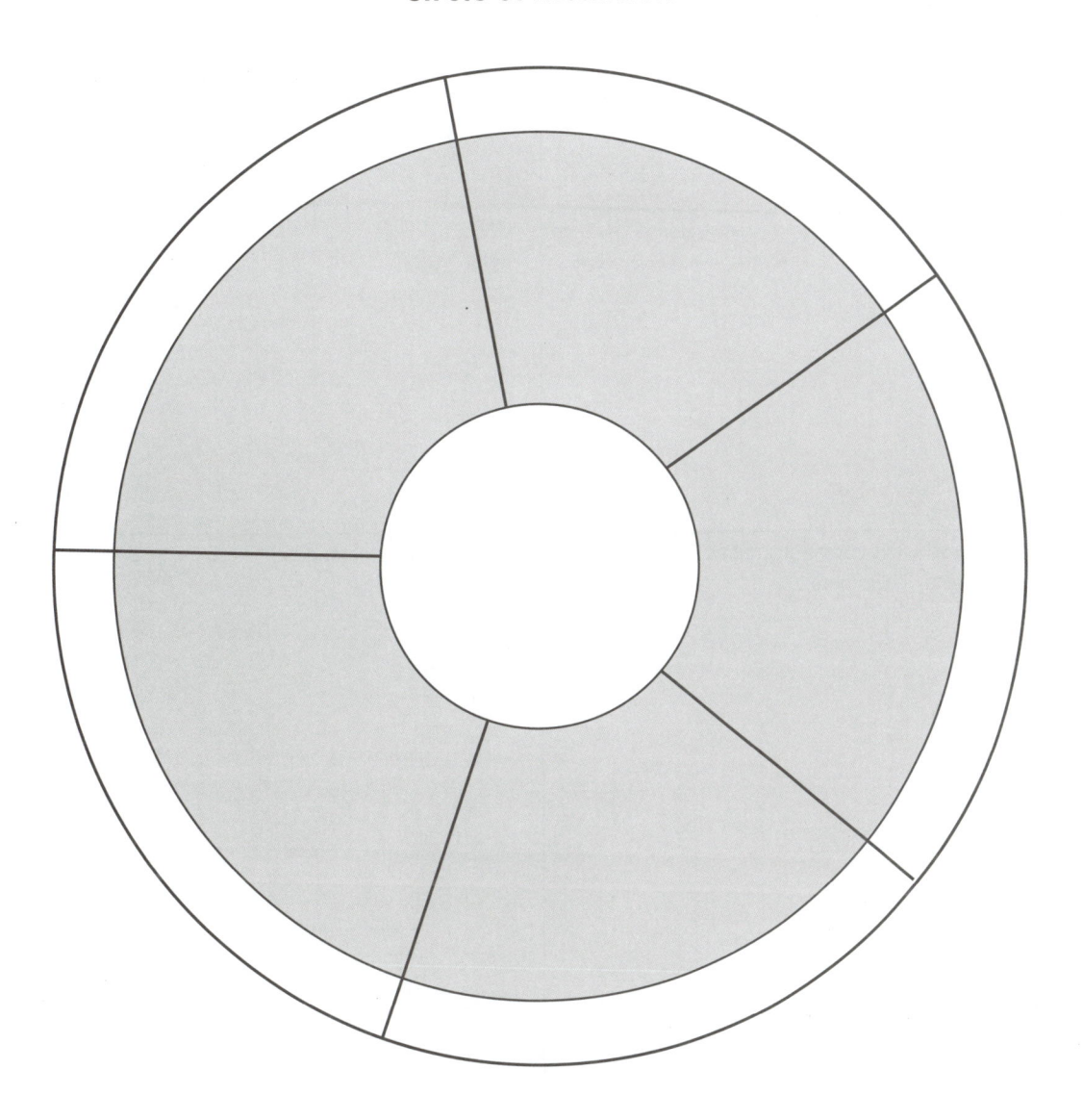

POSITIVE SELF-INTEREST (PSI)

Exercise: Fill in the following chart.

1. Barriers to achieving my self-care action steps…	2. Solutions to address these barriers…
3. Unproductive coping strategies I would like to use less or eliminate…	4. What I will do instead…

CHOOSE YOURSELF STRATEGIES

So far, we've discussed various EQ strategies to improve the EQ area of Choose Yourself. Below are 10 EQ strategies designed to help us continue to grow and develop in this area. These strategies are based upon the concepts we have previously learned.

1. Exercise Optimism

2. Recognize when to dial up and dial down emotions

3. Practice Stop, Think, and Choose

4. Remember anger is a secondary emotion

5. Use self-talk to achieve productive outcomes

6. Practice gratitude

7. Become "gritty" when things get tough

8. Define the consequences of my actions BEFORE acting

9. Accept responsibility

10. Practice self-care

CHOOSE YOURSELF GOAL SETTING

Use the goal setting worksheet to help you achieve or further develop the EQ area of Choose Yourself. To guide your actions, create your step-by-step plan below.

First, list three Choose Yourself concepts (refer to *Course Learning Outcomes* section) that you want to achieve or further develop.

1.

2.

3.

Next, write down an action and deadline for each Choose Yourself concept. For help, refer to the *Choose Yourself Strategies* on the previous page.

1. Action: _____ Deadline: ___/___/___

2. Action: _____ Deadline: ___/___/___

3. Action: _____ Deadline: ___/___/___

Demonstrate one action step you can take utilizing the C.L.E.A.R. (Collaborate, Listen, Empathize, Adapt, and Reward) technique to boost your effectiveness to achieve your set goals.

What challenges might you encounter in trying to achieve your goals?

How might you overcome these challenges to achieve your goals?

Signed: _____ Date: _____

Witness: _____ Date: _____

Chapter Three

GIVE yourself

Notes

EMPATHY

What is Empathy?

Empathy is a deep understanding and feeling toward what other people are experiencing from their point of view. Empathy refers to "I feel *with* you," which is different from "I feel *for* you."

Daniel Goleman (2007) observes, "In today's psychology, the word 'empathy' is used in three distinct senses: knowing another person's feelings, feeling what that person feels, and responding compassionately to another's distress. In short, I notice you, I feel with you, so I act to help you."

Empathy is not about "fixing" the other person's emotional struggles by offering advice or suggestions. Empathy provides a platform for others to feel felt, cared for, and understood without judgment.

Why is Empathy Important?

As humans, we are wired to feel empathy and making the effort to practice empathy more often will create deeper, more meaningful relationships. Research says whether we try to or not, our brains are constantly connecting with others. Marco Iacaboni (2009), neuroscientist at the UCLA Brain Mapping Center, suggests we are hard-wired to feel what others experience as if it were happening to us.

Mirror neurons help explain this powerful connection. Mirror neurons, which are part of the social functioning of our brains, have been defined as a cornerstone of human empathy. They help us understand others by noticing and responding to others' movements and emotions. For example, when we see someone smile, our mirror neurons for smiling fire up as well. It creates a sensation in our own minds of the feeling related with smiling. We are wired to connect.

While we have a natural tendency towards empathy, it's something we can strengthen through intentional practice. Empathy allows us to relate to people's feelings and to see the world through their eyes. By practicing this essential life skill, we can strengthen our relationships and gain long-lasting personal and professional success.

It's important to note that Six Seconds' definition of "Increase Empathy" includes self and others. It's not just about giving empathy to another person. It's building empathy together and self-empathy is often the bigger challenge.

EMPATHY

Exercise: Answer the following questions in each scenario.

Scenario 1

A friend states, "There is so much going on. My day has been overwhelming."

How do you think your friend would feel other than overwhelmed?

How would you feel if you were in this situation?

Provide an empathetic response to your friend.

Scenario 2

A co-worker states, "Last week I fell and now my arm is in pain. My doctor said nothing is broken, but it will take weeks to heal. It's been hard using the computer, but I have a lot of papers to work on."

How do you think your co-worker would feel?

How would you feel if you were in this situation?

Provide an empathetic response to your co-worker.

Scenario 3

Your boss states, "You take too long to do your work. There is no reason it should take so long."

How do you think your boss feels?

How would you feel if you were the boss in this situation?

Provide an empathetic response to your boss.

EMPATHY

Reflective listening is a technique, which shows empathy to another person. Reflective listening refers to listening without interrupting and acting in a positive and polite manner no matter what is said. It also refers to using an even tone of voice and positive body language when making statements that provide reassurance to the other person. Some examples of positive body language include leaning in, making appropriate eye contact, using relaxed and open facial expressions, and keeping an open body position (arms unfolded).

Exercise: Pair up with another individual. Within each pair, one person (*speaker*) will tell the other about an uncomfortable, unfair, or unjust situation in which they were involved. The other person (*listener*) will listen and demonstrate empathy. You will have five minutes to share and then you will switch roles.

Ground Rules:

- The *listener's* purpose is to help the *speaker* explore the situation by reflecting the feelings the speaker experienced and what gave rise to them. Do not attempt to solve the problem!

- To listen and reflect back what they hear, the *listener* can use statements such as:
    - "You feel _____ because _____."
    - "That must have felt _____. It sounds like…"
    - "Tell me more."
    - "I don't quite understand what you are saying." "Can you repeat that?" "Help me understand that."
    - "Are you saying that (repeat speaker's words)?"
    - "Mm," "Uh-huh," "Go on."

Reflective Listening Insights:

A major aspect to increase our empathy includes closely paying attention to others without any distractions. In today's increasingly fast-paced society, practicing empathy takes self-motivation. Here we need to exercise our ability to listen reflectively and understand what is being communicated by the other person, rather than placing judgment or forming our own interpretations. Empathy takes effort that pays off because it leads to more meaningful and deeper relationships.

Notes

HEALTHY RELATIONSHIPS

What is a Healthy Relationship?

A healthy relationship allows both partners to maintain their independence while still feeling supported and connected to each other. The relationship is based upon open communication, mutual respect, trust, honesty, support, and established boundaries.

We all have different relationships with our family, friends, co-workers, and others. As relationships grow, it is normal that disagreements will happen. Healthy relationships do not happen overnight, they take time and dedicated work.

For instance, we may be in a healthy relationship that has unhealthy moments. Other times, we may be in a relationship where we both agree that it is unhealthy and commit to make productive changes together. In those moments of disagreement, how we deal with it is critical to the growth and success of the relationship.

Why Are Healthy Relationships Important?

Six Seconds research of over 75,000 people in 126 countries found a strong, positive relationship between emotional intelligence and healthy relationships. Life is all about relationships. Strong relationships are truly the key to life satisfaction. Embracing healthy communities around us creates for a longer and happier life.

The Harvard Study of Adult Development, almost 80 years old, is one of the most comprehensive studies of wellbeing. Harvard followed the lives of 724 men during the Great Depression. Of the original 724, 19 are still alive today. The results of the study are compelling and amplify that healthy social connections are critical. Robert Waldinger, currently directing the study, reported, "Good relationships keep us happier and healthier. Period. When we gathered together everything we knew about [these participants] at age 50, it wasn't their middle-age cholesterol levels that predicted how they were going to grow old. It was how satisfied they were in their relationships. The people who were the most satisfied in their relationships at age 50 were the healthiest at age 80. Good relationships don't just protect our bodies; they protect our brains."

So, how can we cultivate better relationships? Data suggests that EQ plays a big role in our ability to form and sustain quality relationships.

HEALTHY RELATIONSHIPS

Exercise: Read the paragraph and create your Theatre of Life on the following page.

LIFE IS A THEATRE

Not everyone is healthy enough to have a front row seat in our lives.
There are some people in your life that need to be loved from a DISTANCE.
It's amazing what you can accomplish when you let go of, or at least minimize your time with draining, negative, incompatible, not-going-anywhere relationships/friendships.
Observe the relationships around you. Pay attention.
Which ones lift and which ones lean?
Which ones encourage and which ones discourage?
Which ones are on a path of growth uphill and which ones are going downhill?
When you leave certain people do you feel better or feel worse?
Which ones always have drama or don't really understand, know or appreciate you?
The more you seek quality, respect, growth, peace of mind, love and truth around you...the easier it will become for you to decide who gets to sit in the front row and who should be moved to the balcony of Your Life.
"If you cannot change the people around you, CHANGE the people you are around."
Remember that the people we hang with will have an impact on both our lives and our income. And so we must be careful to choose the people we hang out with, as well as the information with which we feed our minds.
We should not share our dreams with negative people, nor feed our dreams with negative thoughts.
It's your choice and your life... It's up to you who and what you let in it...

-Author Unknown

HEALTHY RELATIONSHIPS

Exercise: Follow these steps to create your Theatre of Life...

1. Think about the people in your life.

2. Think about the various spaces in a theatre.

3. Place the people whom you identified in the appropriate spaces in your theatre.

4. If desired, redesign the outline of this theatre to better express your ideas. Just as stage theatre varies by culture, so does how we build our relationships.

5. Use the following questions to help create your theatre:

    Who's in your front row? Who's in the balcony? Who's in the backstage? Who's on the catwalk? Who's in the orchestra pit? Who's in the control box? Who may be in the parking lot? Who's in the concession stand? Who's in the ticket box? Who's in the dressing room?

Theatre of Life

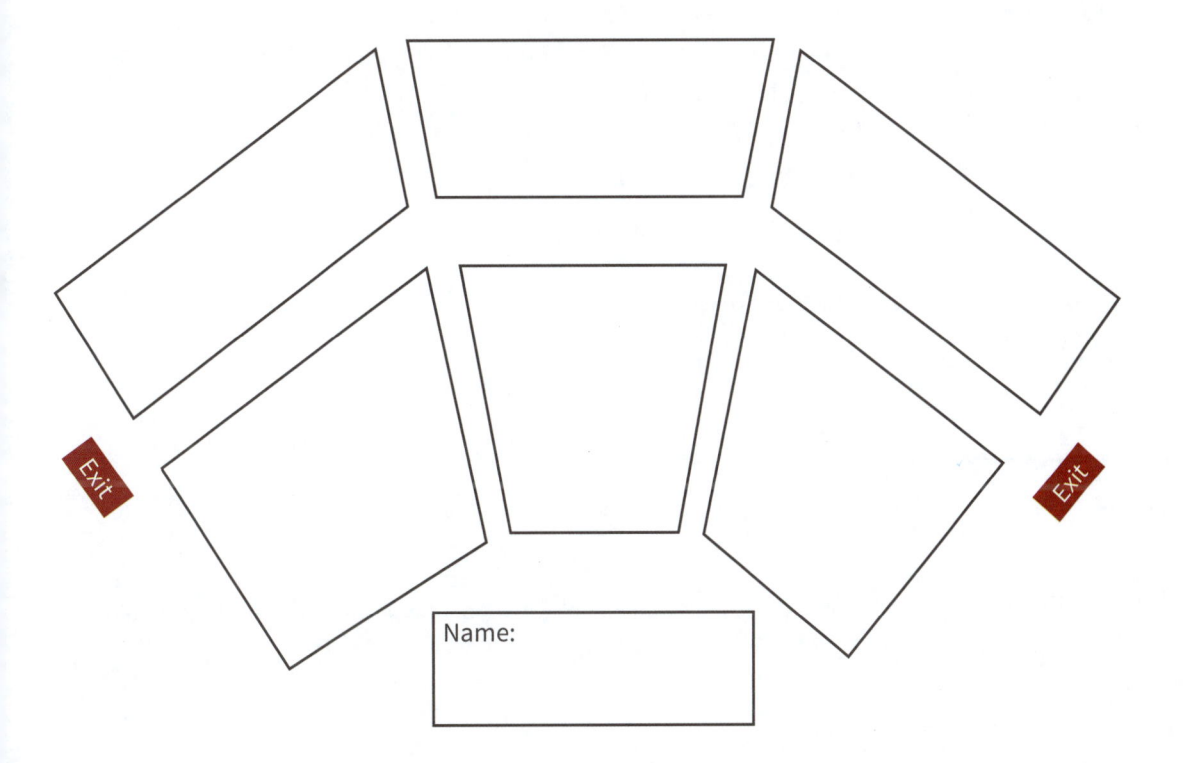

Name:

HEALTHY RELATIONSHIPS

Dr. Chapman, author of *The 5 Love Languages*, developed a theory that everyone has a primary love language. The five love languages describe the way we feel loved and appreciated. We may feel loved differently than how our partners (or other people in our lives) do. According to Dr. Chapman the five love languages are: Words of Affirmation, Acts of Service, Receiving Gifts, Quality Time, and Physical Touch.

Figuring out our love language and the love language of others have reaped benefits. One study determined, for instance, that Chapman's advice was likely to produce certain established "relational maintenance" behaviors that research had previously linked to higher rates of love, satisfaction, commitment, and equity in relationships. So, in theory, it was certainly possible that a couple who applied the principles of the love languages to their day-to-day lives could end up with higher levels of relationship satisfaction (Egbert & Polk, 2006).

This idea encourages us to simply be more attentive to others. It helps us intentionally consider the needs and wants of the other person and then adjust our own behavior to better connect and show appreciation. So, what's your love language? Let's take the test to find out…

Exercise: Visit https://www.5lovelanguages.com/quizzes/to complete the assessment. Determine which assessment best suits you (Teen, Couple's, Singles, or Children's). After taking the assessment, answer the following questions.

1. What is your "preferred language" identified in the quiz?

2. Do you agree with this? Why or why not?

3. From your top two "languages," identify one example from each language of how this is demonstrated in a healthy relationship.

4. If someone uses your least desired "language" with you, how would you feel? How would you respond?

HEALTHY RELATIONSHIPS

Think of someone close to you. Now, take the quiz again but this time take it as though you were them.

5. What is their "preferred language" identified in the quiz?

6. Do you agree with this? Why or why not?

7. How might the information from your quizzes help further develop this relationship?

8. What action steps can you take to apply this information?

9. As an assignment, have this person take the quiz and compare your results. What did you learn?

Notes

EMOTIONAL EXPRESSION

What is emotional expression?

Emotional expression refers to the way in which we communicate experiences and how we influence our relationships. It involves openly expressing our feelings both verbally and nonverbally. Emotional expression is an EQ skill that helps us express our emotions effectively and clearly to others.

Emotional expression is the ability to…

- Accurately identify which emotions we feel rather than using a vague description
- Choose the best way to express an emotion
- Express our feelings clearly and openly versus hinting, implying, or hoping someone will pick up on it
- Have an extensive emotional vocabulary to use
- Express a full range of emotions

Research suggests non-verbal communication is more powerful than verbal communication (Bambaeeroo & Shokrpour, 2017). There is more emphasis on expressing our emotions through non-verbal communication such as facial expressions, body language, gestures, and tone of voice. According to Albert Merhabian's research, the emotional content of communication is carried by:

Face-to-face

- Body language: 55% of the message
- Tonality: 38% of the message
- Words that are used: 7% of the message

Phone

- Body language: between 10-16%
- Tonality: 70% of the message
- Words that are used: 14-20%

EMOTIONAL EXPRESSION

Why is emotional expression important?

We need to recognize how we are expressing our emotions, especially through our non-verbal communication, to ensure we are conveying the appropriate and intended message. The better we can express our emotions, the better our relationships will be with others.

Questions we can ask ourselves to improve our emotional expression are:

- What emotions did I express clearly today and with whom?
- How did I express them?
- What was the outcome when I expressed them in this way?
- Which emotions did I hold back expressing? Why?
- Going forward, how can I express my emotions in order to benefit and improve my relationships?

Emotional expression is an essential skill in order to connect with people. It allows us to communicate more effectively and build stronger relationships, both personally and professionally.

EMOTIONAL EXPRESSION

Have you ever people watched? Many of us enjoy this activity whether it is sitting in a busy airport or watching a movie to observe how people interact and respond. People watching can be more than just a fun activity. It can be a powerful learning experience. If we are having a hard time recognizing our own emotional patterns, we can discover this by observing others.

Exercise: You will be asked to "people watch" and identify another person's non-verbal communication. Follow the directions below:

1. Choose a TV rerun such as *Grey's Anatomy*, *Modern Family*, *Parks and Recreation*, or one that you prefer.
2. Select one of the main characters to observe.
3. Watch the TV rerun for two or three minutes.
4. While watching record your character's non-verbal communication examples in the chart below.

Character's Non-verbal Communication
Facial Expressions
Hand & Body Gestures
Eye Contact
Body Posture
Tone of Voice
Physical Touch
Physical Space
Other:
Other:

EMOTIONAL EXPRESSION

Answer the following questions…

1. Did you record more open or closed non-verbal communication examples? What were the results of this?

2. After completing this activity what is your reaction to the statement of…. *"Non-verbal communication is more powerful than verbal communication"*?

3. How can you apply what you have learned about emotional expression to your personal and professional life?

EMOTIONAL EXPRESSION

Exercise: Read the social media posts below. Next, answer the following questions.

Pessimistic Pete's Social Media Posts

Pessimistic Pete
I give up! Nothing good ever happens to me.

Pessimistic Pete
Ugh, people are annoying me today!

Pessimistic Pete
I really dislike my job. Does anyone know of job openings? I need a new job ASAP!

---

1. If you worked with Pessimistic Pete, how would these messages affect you?

2. Generally, how do people's social media messages affect you?

3. How do you express emotion through your social media platforms?

4. How might this affect others?

5. What are the advantages of social media? Disadvantages?

6. What advice would you give someone who is new to social media?

Notes

FEEDBACK

What is feedback?

Feedback is informational insight given to a person to help improve a previous action. It is not focused on judging or placing blame like criticism. Feedback instead is focused on growth and implementing solutions.

There are two important aspects of feedback which are *giving* and *receiving*. Giving feedback without blaming and receiving feedback without becoming defensive are two major aspects of a successful feedback process.

Why is feedback important?

We often steer away from giving and receiving feedback because it can be difficult and uncomfortable. Withholding feedback is not allowing the other person to obtain honest information that could help improve and strengthen the relationship. Likewise, unwillingness to accept feedback strips us away from personal and professional growth.

Finding the courage and understanding when we are ready to give and accept feedback is crucial. Dr. Brene Brown (2015), research professor, created "The Engaged Feedback Checklist" that provides a recipe for a productive feedback process. This 10-item checklist is simple and straight forward, however sometimes overlooked when providing feedback. Below is Dr. Brown's "Engaged Feedback Checklist".

I know I'm ready to give feedback when…

- I'm ready to sit next to you rather than across from you.
- I'm willing to put the problem in front of us rather than between us (or sliding it toward you).
- I'm ready to listen, ask questions, and accept that I may not fully understand the issue.
- I want to acknowledge what you do well instead of picking apart your mistakes.
- I recognize your strengths and how you can use them to address your challenges.
- I can hold you accountable without shaming or blaming you.

FEEDBACK

- I'm willing to own my part.
- I can genuinely thank you for your efforts rather than criticize you for your failings.
- I can talk about how resolving these challenges will lead to your growth and opportunity.
- I can model the vulnerability and openness that I expect to see from you.

This checklist can increase engagement and productivity of the conversations we have when giving and receiving feedback. When we utilize these EQ strategies and others, we are working towards improved relationships.

Notes

FEEDBACK

One way to provide effective feedback is by using "I" statements. This technique will allow us to communicate while minimizing blaming and criticizing the other person. Follow the four step process:

Step 1: Ask if the person would like your feedback. If they say yes, then move to step 2. If they say no, this is where exploration into the status of your relationship must occur. Simply say, "Help me understand why you don't want my feedback." Go from there. Seek clarity and understanding by using reflective listening. Move to step 2 only when they are ready and willing to receive your feedback. This may take some time.

Step 2: State your feelings honestly but compassionately using: "I feel _____" then the situation. *For example: I feel dissatisfied with the way this is going.* Using "I" statements to honestly express your feelings is honest. The other person can't deny you are feeling this way. It offers a little vulnerability rather than blame.

Step 3: Invite the other person to join you by acknowledging their feelings and asking for collaboration. *For example: How are you feeling? You've also told me that you are not thrilled with this.* Listening to their feelings creates a mutuality. It also helps you bring your empathy forward.

Step 4: Ask how to improve the situation together. *For example: How can we improve this? What can we do to make this better?* Working on it together makes it a collaboration where you are not on opposite sides but standing shoulder-to-shoulder facing a shared challenge.

Turn to the next page to practice applying these four steps...

FEEDBACK

Exercise: After reviewing the example, complete the following "I" statements. For the last box, pick a current event from your life.

Event	Criticism (Reaction)	"I" Statement (Response)
Your friend borrowed your jacket without asking and returned it damaged.	"You are selfish and you ruin my things!"	"I am frustrated that my jacket was damaged." "How are you feeling about this?" "How can we resolve this situation so it doesn't happen again?" "How can we repair our trust in our friendship?"
Your partner does something that annoys you.		
You are working on a group project and one member is not completing tasks assigned.		
You are in an argument with your partner or roommate about your dirty house.		

FEEDBACK

Exercise: Follow the facilitator's lead for this activity.

Let's practice giving feedback…

Scenario 1

Personal Interaction

Scenario 3

Professional Interaction

Scenario 3

Personal or Professional Interaction

Scenario 4

Wild Card (Any Social Interaction)

FEEDBACK

Exercise: Utilize the "Emotoscope Feeling Chart" listed on the following pages, when giving feedback.

Notes

A selection of feeling words...

Category: Mad

Word	Sentence	Purpose	Sensations
Peeved	I feel peeved when people don't do what I want	Focus attention on minor issues	Frowning eyebrow, tight mouth, dry mouth
Disappointed	I feel disappointed because things didn't go as I expected	Focus attention on something you want to change	Frowning eyebrow, tight mouth, dry mouth
Miffed	I feel miffed because someone hurt my feelings	Focus attention on a small but significant problem	Frowning eyebrow, tight mouth, dry mouth
Annoyed	I feel annoyed because things are not going my way	Focus attention on a problem you've ignored	Agitation, headache, tense muscles
Irritated	I feel irritated because this problem keeps coming up	Focus attention on something that goes against your beliefs	Agitation, headache, tense muscles
Critical	I feel critical because people are not doing their part	Focus attention on a relationship problem	Agitation, headache, tense muscles
Angry	I feel angry because I can't do what I want	Focus attention on something you want to change	Warm hands, fast pulse, narrow eyes, tense shoulders
Vindictive	I feel vindictive because I want to punish someone	Focus attention on something you might need to oppose	Warm hands, fast pulse, narrow eyes, tense shoulders
Boiling	I am boiling because someone's keeping me from my goals	Focus attention on a problem	Warm hands, fast pulse, narrow eyes, tense shoulders
Fuming	I am fuming because this person keeps interfering	Focus attention on a lasting issue	Heat, fast pulse, red
Livid	I am livid because nothing is changing	Focus attention on something that goes against your values	Heat, fast pulse, red
Infuriated	I feel infuriated because people are in my way	Focus attention on a significant, persistent issue	Heat, fast pulse, red
Outraged	I feel outraged because someone is totally wrong	Focus attention on something that violates your values	Boiling heat, rapid heart, sweaty palms
Furious	I feel furious because something is blocking my way	Focus attention on something very serious	Boiling heat, rapid heart, sweaty palms
Explosive	I feel explosive because there's so much in my way	Focus attention on a dangerous problem	Boiling heat, rapid heart, sweaty palms

KNOW CHOOSE GIVE PARTICIPANT WORKBOOK

Category: Sad

Word	Sentence	Purpose	Sensations
Insignificant	I feel insignificant and people don't know or care about me.	Challenge you to find your place	Downturned eyes, frown, soft shoulders
Overwhelmed	I feel overwhelmed because too much is happening.	Challenge you to set priorities	Downturned eyes, frown, soft shoulders
Withdrawn	I feel withdrawn because the world out there doesn't feel safe.	Help you recover your energy	Downturned eyes, frown, soft shoulders
Lonely	I feel lonely because people don't reach out to me.	Help you consider the strength of your relationships	Far away look, heaviness, slow pulse
Disturbed	I feel disturbed because something is not right.	Help you clarify your values	Far away look, heaviness, slow pulse
Gloomy	I feel gloomy because I have lost my purpose.	Help you identify problems	Far away look, heaviness, slow pulse
Sad	I feel sad because something is being taken away from me.	Help you recognize what you care about	Moist eyes, head down, body turning inward.
Discouraged	I feel discouraged because I can't seem to get what I want.	Challenge you to check your level of commitment	Moist eyes, head down, body turning inward.
Defeated	I feel defeated because I have tried and lost again.	Challenge you to face a failure and learn	Moist eyes, head down, body turning inward.
Heartbroken	I feel heartbroken because I have given of myself and feel empty.	Challenge you to clarify what you want in a relationship	Tears, arms folded in, head down.
Miserable	I feel miserable because I have lost trust in people important to me.	Challenge you to confront a big problem	Tears, arms folded in, head down.
Anguished	I feel anguished because I have lost my direction.	Challenge you to recognize a major change you need to make	Tears, arms folded in, head down.
Grief-stricken	I feel grief-stricken because I have lost something/someone important in my life.	Help you recognize how much you love someone/something	Wet eyes/face, hands to face, devastated
Devastated	I feel devastated because I don't see any options in my future.	Challenge you to confront a failure	Wet eyes/face, hands to face, devastated
Distraught	I feel distraught because I can't decide what to do next.	Challenge you to confront something terribly uncomfortable	Wet eyes/face, hands to face, devastated

Category: Glad

Word	Sentence	Purpose	Sensations
Peaceful	I feel peaceful because the world is as it should be.	Reinforce your sense of connection	Eyes relaxed, head held high, relaxed body.
Content	I feel content because I have chosen a direction that gives me value & purpose.	Reinforce the value of your efforts	Eyes relaxed, head held high, relaxed body.
Confident	I feel confident because I know I can meet my goals	Strengthen your resolve and commitment	Eyes relaxed, head held high, relaxed body.
Pleased	I feel pleased because I have accomplished my goals.	Remind you of what you like	Eyebrows raised, upturned mouth, shoulders back.
Happy	I feel happy because I am satisfied with myself.	Help you pay attention to what's good in life	Eyebrows raised, upturned mouth, shoulders back.
Hopeful	I feel hopeful because good things are coming	Energize you to persevere through challenge	Eyebrows raised, upturned mouth, shoulders back.
Delighted	I feel delighted because the outcome of my choices bring me joy.	Energize you to share joy	Eyes open, smiling, tall/proud posture
Cheerful	I feel cheerful because I am settled and satisfied.	Remind you that the world is a wonderful place	Eyes open, smiling, tall/proud posture
Joyful	I feel joyful because I am getting what I really want!	Remind you of what matters most to you	Eyes open, smiling, tall/proud posture
Thrilled	I feel thrilled because I have had a fortunate outcome to my actions.	Energize you to risk and grow	Eyes looking up, increased pulse, active arms.
Ecstatic	I feel ecstatic because I am doing and being exactly what gives me pleasure.	Energize you to stay connected and fully alive	Eyes looking up, increased pulse, active arms.
Exuberant	I feel exuberant because I am pleased and surprised by my gains.	Energize you to motivate and engage others	Eyes looking up, increased pulse, active arms.
Wacky	I feel wacky and full of energy for what lies ahead.	Help you innovate and take risks	Expressive eyes, warmth, active body.
Goofy	I feel goofy and ready to play with great abandon.	Help you release energy and renew	Expressive eyes, warmth, active body.
Hilarious	I feel hilarious and full of vim & vigor!	Help you release energy and innovate	Expressive eyes, warmth, active body.

Category: afraid

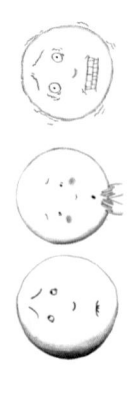

Word	Sentence	Purpose	Sensations
Insecure	I feel insecure because I have lost my confidence.	Consider your own strengths	Eyebrows tight, eyes squinted, agitation.
Timid	I feel timid because I am unsure of myself.	Consider the kinds of relationships you want	Eyebrows tight, eyes squinted, agitation.
Shy	I feel shy because I might not fit in	Consider how you fit in	Eyebrows tight, eyes squinted, agitation.
Anxious	I feel anxious because I am not sure how things will work out	Focus attention on potential problems	Eyes wide open, frown, knot in tummy.
Lost	I feel lost because I don't know where I want to go	Focus attention on next steps	Eyes wide open, frown, knot in tummy.
Worried	I feel worried because I am unwilling to face something.	Focus attention on potential problems	Eyes wide open, frown, knot in tummy.
Astonished	I feel astonished because I was caught off guard.	Focus attention on the unexpected	Eyes open, open mouth, hands close to face/body.
Startled	I feel startled because I am being asked to do something new & unfamiliar.	Focus attention on something new	Eyes open, open mouth, hands close to face/body.
Uncertain	I feel uncertain because I don't know if the situation will work out	Focus attention on your level of commitment	Eyes open, open mouth, hands close to face/body.
Frightened	I feel frightened because there is danger in the near future.	Focus attention on a risk	Hard to focus, clenched jaw, cold & sweaty
Horrified	I feel horrified because the shock of the news hit me hard.	Focus attention on something that you don't want	Hard to focus, clenched jaw, cold & sweaty
Terror-stricken	I feel terror-stricken because what I love is in danger	Focus attention on serious risk	Hard to focus, clenched jaw, cold & sweaty
Terrified	I feel terrified because something awful is coming	Focus attention on danger	Squinty eyes, shaking body, shortness of breath.
Panicky	I feel panicky because I am not sure what to prepare myself for.	Focus attention on what you need to do next	Squinty eyes, shaking body, shortness of breath.
Petrified	I feel petrified because I don't want to regret any decision that I have to make.	Focus attention on a serious danger	Squinty eyes, shaking body, shortness of breath.

Emotoscope is a free online feeling finder | www.6seconds.org/feel | by Joshua Freedman & Marilynn Jorgensen
Faces are from the eMotion Cards ©The eMotion Company, available from www.6seconds.org/store or amazon.com

INDEPENDENCE

What is independence?

Independence means being self-empowered and living in our own positive self-interest (PSI). It means taking responsibility for our own emotional, physical, spiritual, personal, professional, and psychological needs. Through independence we will build purpose, direction, and trust for ourselves.

This is not being selfish or insensitive. It's having the ability to consider others while assessing our own beliefs and values. Being independent contributes to the ability to make decisions and to stand on our own two feet but most importantly to trust our own judgment.

Why is independence important?

When we take responsibility for our own life and our own choices, it is extremely empowering. It's when we put our happiness in the hands of others, it becomes dangerous. Independence is neither isolation from others nor rejection of support. Most great achievements we experience in life involve the role of many others in the background.

Likewise, independence leads us to interdependence. Two people who are able to function independently, share responsibility equally, and take responsibility for their own feelings, actions, and contributions to the relationship is known as interdependency. Relationships that are built based on interdependence leads to healthy and satisfying long-term outcomes. Interdependence gives us strength to support others while focusing on our own personal growth.

INDEPENDENCE

Exercise: We will use TFA to dive deeper into the concept of independence. You will be asked to "people watch" and identify another person's thoughts, feelings, and actions.

To start:

1. Watch "Helicopter Parents: The lengths parents go to pamper & please their kids", visit https://www.youtube.com/watch?v=ufEfeDP7vBA.

2. Choose either the Mother or the Son to observe and record.

Next:

3. Record the person's potential thoughts. Write down a defining phrase or word that represents the thought, not the entire thought. For example, if the person is thinking about how stressed they are because of everything going on this week, simply write "stressed".

4. Record the person's potential feelings. Try to record <u>every</u> feeling the person is experiencing. Use The EQ Feeling Chart as a reference.

5. Record at least two or three actions displayed by the person.

Person's Thoughts	Person's Feelings	Person's Actions

INDEPENDENCE

Answer the following questions…

1. What are the short-term consequences of the person's TFA?

2. What are the long-term consequences of the person's TFA?

3. How would you have handled this situation?

4. Describe a time when you behaved too dependent or independent (for example, either asking someone to do something for you when you could have done it yourself or not accepting help when actually needing it).

5. What were your thoughts?

6. What were your feelings?

7. What were the short-term consequences?

8. What were the long-term consequences?

9. What could you have changed to create a better outcome?

INDEPENDENCE

Exercise: Answer the following questions.

1. What are some examples in which you do not believe people are acting independently? What is the impact of this?

2. When is it easy and when is it hard to be independent?

3. What are specific choices you can make to become more independent in your current environment?

4. How do independence and decision-making relate?

5. How do confidence and independence relate?

INDEPENDENCE

6. If someone in your life is not allowing you your independence, what are some things you can do? How does culture and family history play a role?

7. What are some examples you might have that illustrate being dependent?

8. Sometimes people can try to be TOO independent and fail to take care of people in their lives. When have you done this?

9. A balanced state of independence could be called, "interdependence." What would it mean for you to develop a healthy interdependence with the people in your life?

Notes

COMMUNICATION STYLES

What are commmunication styles?

Communication styles are ways in which we communicate verbal and non-verbal messages. There are various communication styles including: passive, aggressive, passive-aggressive, and assertive.

They are defined as:

Passive: a style of avoiding expressing opinions or feelings.

Aggressive: a style of expressing opinions or feelings in a way that violates the rights of others.

Passive-aggressive: a style of expressing opinions or feelings in a subtle, indirect, or behind-the-scenes way.

Assertive: a style of clearly expressing opinions or feelings with preserving the rights of others.

Why are communication styles important?

We all have a particular style of communicating. Do you know what yours is? What are its strengths and weaknesses? How does it compare to the styles of others?

It is important to be aware of our communication style and the communication style of others in order to determine how we can respond, or not respond, effectively. Picking the wrong style for a certain audience, shuts down the conversation. It can damage our relationships.

Learning to be flexible around our preferred communication style allows others to hear us effectively. It can strengthen our relationships and provide opportunities for growth and possibility.

COMMUNICATION STYLES

Exercise: After reviewing the chart below, circle the communication style(s) that you use most frequently during conflicts with others.

	Passive	Aggressive	Passive-Aggressive	ASSERTIVE
Style	I lose, you win	I win, you lose	I lose, you lose	I win, you win
What I see	Poor eye contact Hunched posture	Tense body language Pointing	Rolling of the eyes Closed off body language	Good eye contact Confident posture
What I hear	"Sorry…" "This is not important, but…"	"You…" "That's not my problem."	"I can't believe she did that." (underneath their breath)	"I…" "No…" Open ended questions
Results	They do not respond, but still feel hurt. They allow others to take advantage of them.	They blame others and don't take responsibility for themselves. They violate the rights of others.	They avoid direct confrontation. They become defensive.	They respect others and listen respectfully. They take responsibility for themselves.

COMMUNICATION STYLES

Exercise: Answer the following questions.

1. When might it be appropriate to be a passive communicator?

2. When might it be appropriate to be a passive-aggressive communicator?

3. When might it be appropriate to be an aggressive communicator?

4. What would happen if the two people communicating were both using the passive style? (Answer considering both the process and the end result.)

5. What would happen if the two people communicating were both using an aggressive style? (Answer considering both the process and the end result.)

COMMUNICATION STYLES

6. What would happen if the two people communicating were both using a passive-aggressive style? (Answer considering both the process and the end result.)

7. What would happen if one person communicating uses a passive style and the other uses an aggressive style? (Answer considering both the process and the end result.)

8. What happens if the two people communicating both use an assertive style? (Answer considering both the process and the end result.)

9. Should the assertive style always be used? When and where might another style be appropriate?

PROBLEM OWNERSHIP

WHAT IS PROBLEM OWNERSHIP?

Problem ownership refers to a process of determining who "owns" the problem and how to respond in a solution-focused approach.

Problem ownership encourages us not to feel responsible for the problems of others. We can learn to show empathy and listen with care without feeling the need to "fix" other people's problems.

WHY IS PROBLEM OWNERSHIP IMPORTANT?

A problem must be clearly identified in order to effectively create a solution. As simple as this may sound, we often move into a "fixing" mode immediately without a clear understanding of what is actually happening and understanding whose problem it really is. We tend to take on other people's problems when actually the problem is not ours at all.

Applying problem ownership prevents misunderstanding and arguments in relationships. It is a vital strategy used to help determine the best possible approach to a problem that occurs.

PROBLEM OWNERSHIP

A widely cited approach to resolving conflict effectively comes from Thomas Gordon's Problem Ownership Model. Gordon (2003) explains resolving conflict starts with practicing **problem ownership**, or deciding whose problem a behavior or conflict it really is. When using this model, we don't attempt to solve someone else's problem. Instead, we try to determine whose problem it is and how to best respond in the situation.

Exercise: Follow the facilitator's lead in filling out the Problem Ownership Model.

Who Owns the Problem?

How do I Respond to the Problem?

PROBLEM OWNERSHIP

Exercise: Circle who owns the problem and how to appropriately respond in the following scenarios.

1. A friend tells you she is worried about not meeting an important deadline.

    Other   **No**   I   **We**

    How would you appropriately respond?

2. Your partner often makes a mess in the kitchen and leaves you the responsibility for cleaning.

    Other   **No**   I   **We**

    How would you appropriately respond?

3. Your friend is learning to play the guitar and asks you to listen to the chords he has learned.

    Other   **No**   I   **We**

    How would you appropriately respond?

4. Your supervisors expresses concerns with your performance. You express concerns with the work conditions, which are affecting your performance.

    Other   **No**   I   **We**

    How would you appropriately respond?

Notes

NEGOTIATION

What is Negotiation?

Negotiation is an attempt to bring about cooperative behavior in our relationships while maintaining a high level of respect. It is a way in which we settle differences and reach a compromise while practicing empathy towards others.

In addition, negotiation is the process of using our emotions to reach a constructive agreement. One common misconception of negotiating is that it is better to leave emotions out of it. Dr. Dan Shapiro (2017), Founder and Director of the Harvard International Negotiation Program, says it is impossible, "One can try to leave emotions out, but they are relentlessly there, for better or worse. You cannot avoid emotions any more than you can avoid thoughts. Given that reality, why not use them to be helpful?"

Why is Negotiation Important?

In times of conflict, we play into the myth of winning. When we think "me versus you" it fuels a "colorful set of stubborn emotions." When our state of mind reflects this, it means no matter who "wins" the fight, we lose. It feels better to win, literally. Freedman and Roitman (2019) reports "the brain gives itself a dopamine reward for being certain. We're addicted to righteous – to winning."

When we realize that winning the battle may mean losing the war, we become more realistic about employing the win-win model. Utilizing EQ skills, such as empathy, can take us from a win-lose approach, to a win-win approach. Win-win negotiations can allow both parties to feel that they made a beneficial compromise and that neither is the "loser." This approach leads us to produce creative options, acceptable solutions, and opportunities to develop our relationships further.

NEGOTIATION

Exercise: Follow the facilitator's lead in filling out the effective steps to negotiate.

NEGOTIATION

Exercise: Follow the facilitator's lead for this activity.

Let's practice negotiating…

Scenario 1: Personal Situation

Scenario 3: Professional Situation

Scenario 3: Personal or Professional Situation

Scenario 4: Wild Card (Any Social Situation)

Notes

CONFLICT MANAGEMENT

What is conflict management?

Conflict management is the process of people actively working together through a problem in order to establish a productive outcome. It is the practice of being able to identify conflict when it arises and the ability to handle it wisely.

Why is conflict management important?

Conflict is unavoidable and it happens every day. There is no such thing as a relationship without conflict. Whether it involves a relationship at school, work, or home, most of our days are spent in some type of conflict. Conflict is normal and, in fact, healthy if handled appropriately. Learning to handle conflict in productive ways is vital.

At points, we may approach the conflict as a "me versus you" mindset. This could set off various unpleasant feelings, which can make conflict hard to overcome. Shifting our state of mind from "me versus you" to "we are in this together" makes that person our ally instead of our enemy. In Aikido, a Japanese martial art, a central principle is to stand shoulder-to-shoulder facing the issue together. This can help redirect the energy in the conflict.

Here's how we can use KCG to effectively manage conflict…

Know Yourself: tune in…into yourself and your emotions.

Choose Yourself: de-escalate…get out of the "emotionally hijacked" state.

Give Yourself: step so you both feel you are standing shoulder-to-shoulder…connect with emotions and a larger purpose to focus on what truly matters.

When we apply EQ skills in a conflict, such as displaying empathy, providing effective feedback, and applying impulse control, we can move forward in our relationships with solutions in hand. Handling conflict wisely produces an outlet for our relationships to grow stronger and become long-lasting.

CONFLICT MANAGEMENT

Exercise: We all handle conflict differently. Some of the strategies we use may be determined by factors such as the environment and our personality. However, generally there are five major styles of conflict, which include Accommodating, Avoiding, Compromising, Collaborating, and Competing.

There isn't necessarily one conflict style that is better than another, it just depends on the context in which they are used. Yet, we all gravitate to a particular conflict style. After reading the explanations of each style, circle the style(s) that you use most frequently when dealing with conflict.

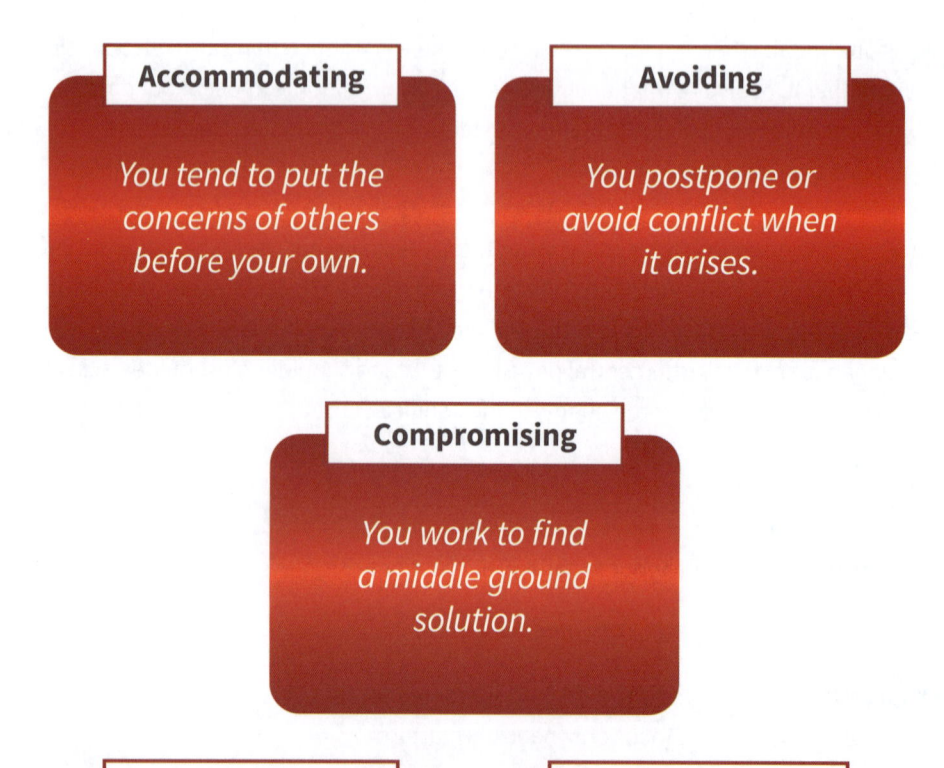

Accommodating
You tend to put the concerns of others before your own.

Avoiding
You postpone or avoid conflict when it arises.

Compromising
You work to find a middle ground solution.

Collaborating
You work to find solutions that meet the needs of all parties.

Competing
You take a firm position and reject the perspectives and opinions of others.

CONFLICT MANAGEMENT

Exercise: Answer the following questions.

1. What are the advantages and disadvantages of each conflict management style?

2. Why is it important to utilize all conflict management styles?

3. Which style is difficult for you to work with? How can you overcome this?

4. How does this activity help explain different conflict situations you have encountered?

CONFLICT MANAGEMENT

Exercise: Follow the facilitator's lead for this activity.

Let's practice conflict management skills…

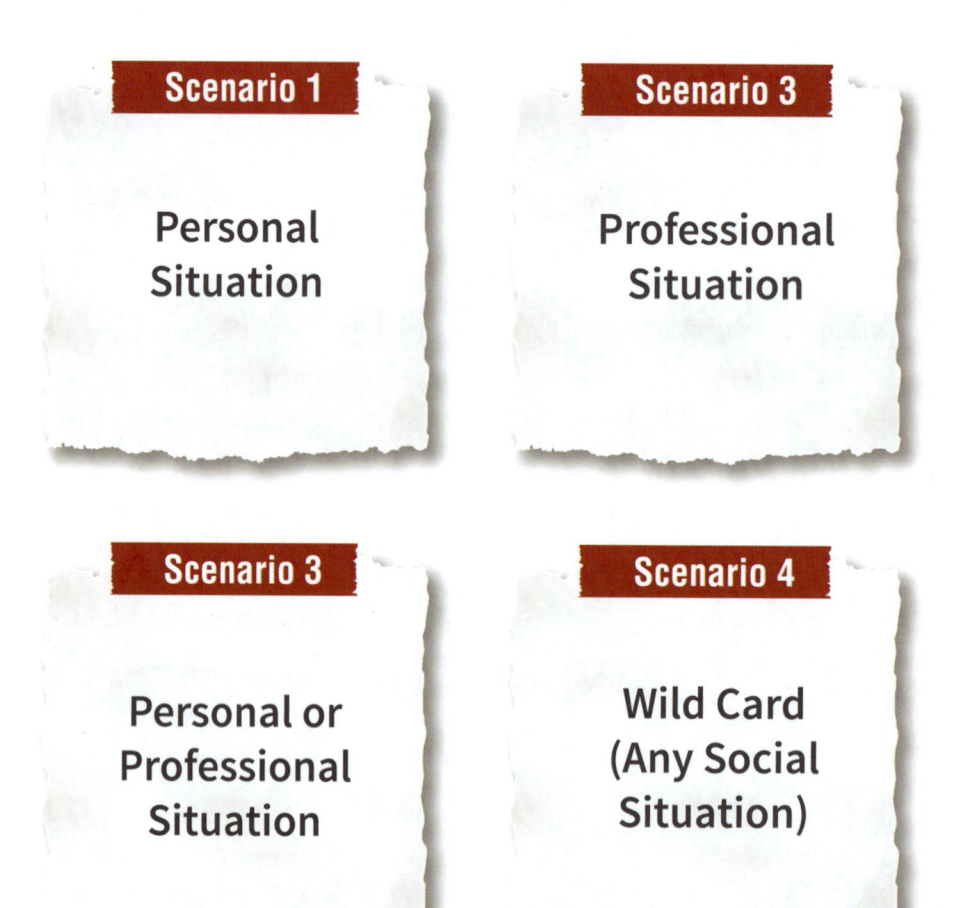

Scenario 1

Personal Situation

Scenario 3

Professional Situation

Scenario 3

Personal or Professional Situation

Scenario 4

Wild Card (Any Social Situation)

NOBLE GOAL

What is a Noble Goal?

A Noble Goal is a brief and compelling statement of purpose that helps us evaluate our choices. Beyond a "mission statement," a Noble Goal encompasses all aspects of our life (personal, work, community, etc.) and inspires us to live our best life. A Noble Goal connects our daily choices with our overarching sense of purpose.

A Noble Goal is a type of purpose statement – not just the what, but also the why and how. It is not intended as an "action plan," but a guide to remind us what is important. To serve as a benchmark for decision-making, and to support us to step out of reacting and into responding with purpose.

Why is having a Noble Goal important?

When we are clear about our Noble Goal, we feel compelled to pay fierce attention to our daily choices to ensure we are not undermining our life's purpose. Pursuing a Noble Goal facilitates integrity and ethical behavior, which helps us maintain focus, inspire others, and access our full potential and power.

Finding and following purpose is quite literally a matter of life and death. A recent study published in the *Journal of the American Medical Association* found that having a life purpose significantly decreased a person's risk of dying, even more so than typical health risks like drinking, smoking or not exercising regularly (Alimujiang, Wiensch, Boss, Fleischer, Mondul, McLean, & Pearce, 2019).

Today, there is a growing body of evidence on the connection between purpose and wellbeing. Alan Rozanski, a professor at the Icahn School of Medicine at Mount Sinai, who has conducted his own research into life purpose and physical health, reported that the results speak for themselves, "The need for meaning and purpose is No. 1. It's the deepest driver of wellbeing there is" (Gordon, 2019).

NOBLE GOAL

What makes you, you? What's your story? When developing your Noble Goal, it helps to ask yourself those questions. Developing a Noble Goal can be challenging, so Six Seconds developed guidelines to help you start this process.

> A Noble Goal typically contains an action verb (expressing how to pursue it) and a goal of what you want to add to the world.
>
> According to Six Seconds' definition, for a goal to qualify as a Noble Goal, these five criteria must be present:
>
> 1. **Not complete in your lifetime** – It is enduring and inspiring, something beyond the daily struggle. This helps you maintain a long-term focus so you can avoid the confusion of short-term thinking.
>
> 2. **Points outward** – While you will benefit, the focus is on others. This helps you maintain an expansive vision.
>
> 3. **Integrates different domains** – It encompasses all dimensions of your life; serving your noble goal in one domain (such as work) supports you in all others (such as family).
>
> 4. **Gets you out of bed** – It motivates and inspires you at a deep level; this helps you to have the energy when the going gets tough.
>
> 5. **No one made less** – No one has to be "less than" or "wrong" for you to pursue your Noble Goal; this helps you stay out of ego and power struggle.
>
> **Examples might be:**
>
> *Empowering lives of intention and purpose*
>
> *Supporting myself and others to live in truth*
>
> *Sparking the awareness of the power of choice*
>
> *Inspiring moments of optimism and happiness*
>
> Which criteria are inspiring you?

NOBLE GOAL

Clarifying your unique strengths, values, passions, and purpose can give you direction in creating your Noble Goal.

Exercise: Fill out the statements below to start this process. Next, attempt to create your Noble Goal based on your responses.

Words associated with me:

My top three core values:

Things I'm passionate about:

Things I'm doing to fuel my passion:

My top three strengths:

The vision for my future:

What I want to add to the world:

My Noble Goal…

_____
_____
_____
_____

Notes

GIVE YOURSELF STRATEGIES

So far, we've discussed various EQ strategies to improve the EQ area of Give Yourself. Below are 10 EQ strategies designed to help us continue to grow and develop in this area. These strategies are based upon the concepts we have previously learned.

1. Invest in my relationships

2. Be an expert at reading people

3. Accept giving and receiving feedback

4. Check-in with others

5. Discover my independence and interdependence

6. Communicate effectively by using the appropriate style

7. Identify whose problem it is

8. Hold a "win-win" attitude

9. Handle conflict effectively by using the appropriate style

10. Pursue my Noble Goal

GIVE YOURSELF GOAL SETTING

Use the goal setting worksheet to help you achieve or further develop in EQ area of Give Yourself. To guide your actions, create your step-by-step plan below.

First, list three Give Yourself concepts (refer to *Course Learning Outcomes* section) that you want to achieve or further develop.

1.

2.

3.

Next, write down an action and deadline for each Give Yourself concept. For help, refer to the *Give Yourself Strategies* on the previous page.

1. Action: Deadline: ___/___/___

2. Action: Deadline: ___/___/___

3. Action: Deadline: ___/___/___

Demonstrate one action step using the C.L.E.A.R. (Collaborate, Listen, Empathy, Adapt, and Reward) technique to boost your effectiveness to achieve your set goals.

What challenges might you encounter in trying to achieve your goals?

How might you overcome these challenges to achieve your goals?

Signed: _____ Date: _____

Witness: _____ Date: _____

Chapter Four
Positive Action Plan

Notes

POSITIVE ACTION PLAN

You have been asked to stretch yourself in self-awareness, self-management, and self-direction. More than likely it hasn't been easy, but hopefully it has been rewarding.

Exercise: This final exercise will encourage you to continue to stretch yourself and to grow. It will help you set new goals for yourself and for your relationships. Go back and review your developed personal goals in each EQ area of Know Yourself, Choose Yourself, and Give Yourself. Expand these goals by completing your Positive Action Plan.

	Know Yourself	Choose Yourself	Give Yourself
What growth did I experience?			
What do I still want to work on?			
How will I put these into action?			
Why are these goals important to me and others in my life?			

POSITIVE ACTION PLAN

INVITATION

Congratulations for completing this workbook! We hope this has been a rewarding experience. Take a moment and consider the many important skills you have explored and practiced. We encourage you to practice every day. The more you practice emotional intelligence skills, the more developed the brain's neural pathways related to EQ becomes.

So what's next? One way to keep EQ skills fresh is to form or join a group in which members teach and learn from each other. We would like for you to join the Six Seconds Network, the largest EQ community of practitioners in the world.

To join and actively participate:

- Visit 6sec.org/join
- Follow Six Seconds social media account for online courses (6sec.org/connect)
- Participate in an EQ café in your area
- Take the SEI EQ assessment and have a 1-1 coaching debrief
- Participate in a training course to further develop your own EQ
- Spread EQ – share with others, invite people, make your own circles
- Share your learning by finding your three most valuable lessons from this workbook and posting them on social media to discuss with others

What would you like to do next?

Notes

SPECIAL THANK YOU

I have to start by thanking the University of Dubuque for understanding the importance of providing explicit and meaningful emotional intelligence (EQ) education in higher education. Through their mission, I was given the opportunity to develop a campus-wide EQ program that included the early stages of this curriculum.

Additionally, thank you to Six Seconds for welcoming me with open arms to the largest EQ community in the world. I want to give a special thank you to the editors from the Six Seconds community: Julie Binter, Amanda Crawford, Robert Ingram, Dr. Anabel Jensen, Cherilyn Leet, Michael Miller, Dr. Yoshi Newman, and Liliana Selva for their help and dedication along the way. Their expertise, positive energy, and commitment have brought this workbook to life. Thank you for your continuous guidance and support.

Finally to you, the learner of this workbook, thank you! I am grateful for the time you spent on developing and growing your EQ skills and sharing it with others. Together we are working towards a billion people practicing EQ.

- Dr. Liza D. Johnson

Notes

REFERENCES

Alimujiang, A., Wiensch, A., Boss, J., Fleischer, N. L., Mondul, A. M., McLean, K., ... & Pearce, C. L. (2019). Association between life purpose and mortality among US adults older than 50 years. *JAMA network open*, *2*(5), e194270-e194270.

American Heart Association. (2014). Stress and heart health. Retrieved from https://www.heart.org/en/healthy-living/healthy-lifestyle/stress-management/stress-and-heart-health

American Psychological Association. (2017). Stress in America: The state of our nation. Retrieved from https://www. apa. org/news/press/releases/stress/2017/state-nation. pdf.

Aschbacher, K., O'Donovan, A., Wolkowitz, O. M., Dhabhar, F. S., Su, Y., & Epel, E. (2013). Good stress, bad stress and oxidative stress: insights from anticipatory cortisol reactivity. *Psychoneuroendocrinology*, *38*(9), 1698-1708.

Bambaeeroo, F., & Shokrpour, N. (2017). The impact of the teachers' non-verbal communication on success in teaching. *Journal of advances in medical education & professionalism*, *5*(2), 51.

Bariso, J. (2018). *EQ Applied: The real-world guide to emotional intelligence*. Smashwords Edition.

Brackett, M. (2019). *Permission to feel: Unlocking the power of emotions to help our kids, ourselves, and our society thrive* (First ed.). New York: Celadon Books.

Bradberry, T., Greaves, J. (2009). *Emotional intelligence 2.0*. Grand Haven, MI: Brilliance Audio.

Brown, B. (host). (2020, April 14). *Dr. Marc Brackett and Brené Brown on "Permission to Feel"* [Audio podcast]. Retrieved from https://brenebrown.com/podcast/dr-marc-brackett-and-brene-on-permission-to-feel/

Brown, B. (2012). *Daring greatly : How the courage to be vulnerable transforms the way we live, love, parent, and lead*. New York, NY: Gotham Books.

Burton, Neel (2015). Self-confidence versus self-esteem. Retrieved from https://www.psychologytoday.com/us/blog/hide-and-seek/201510/self-confidence- versus-self-esteem

Canfield, J. (1990). Improving students' self-esteem. *Educational Leadership*, *48*(1), 48-50.

Chapman, G. (n.d.) *5 love languages quizzes* [Webpage]. Retrieved from https://www.5lovelanguages.com/quizzes/

Cobb-Clark, D. A., Dahmann, S., Kamhöfer, D., & Schildberg-Hörisch, H. (2019). Self-control: Determinants, life outcomes and intergenerational implications.

REFERENCES

Collaborative for Academic, Social, and Emotional Learning (2019). The CASEL guide to school-wide social and emotional learning. Chicago: CASEL. Retrieved from https://schoolguide.casel.org/

Cohen, R., Bavishi, C., & Rozanski, A. (2016). Purpose in life and its relationship to all-cause mortality and cardiovascular events: A meta-analysis. *Psychosomatic medicine*, *78*(2), 122-133.

Denton, W. H., Johnson, S. M., & Burleson, B. R. (2009). Emotion-focused therapy–therapist fidelity scale (EFT-TFS): Conceptual development and content validity. *Journal of couple & relationship therapy*, *8*(3), 226-246.

Duckworth, A. (2016). *Grit : The power of passion and perseverance*. New York, NY: Scribner.

Duckworth, A. L., Peterson, C., Matthews, M. D., & Kelly, D. R. (2007). Grit: perseverance and passion for long-term goals. *Journal of personality and social psychology*, *92*(6), 1087.

Dweck, C. S. (2008). *Mindset: The new psychology of success*. Random House Digital, Inc.

Egbert, N., & Polk, D. (2006). Speaking the language of relational maintenance: A validity test of Chapman's Five Love Languages. *Communication Research Reports*, *23*(1), 19-26.

Emmons, R. (2008). *Thanks! : How practicing gratitude can make you happier*. New York: Houghton Mifflin.

Flade, P., Asplund, J., & Elliot, G. (2015). *Employees who use their strengths outperform those who don't*. Gallup. Retrieved from https://www.gallup.com/workplace/236561/employees-strengths-outperform-don.aspx

Frankl, Victor (1992). Man's Search for Meaning. (4th ed.). Boston, MA: Beacon Press.

Freedman, J. (2020). *EQ practitioner certification manual*. Freedom, CA: Six Seconds Emotional Intelligence Press.

Freedman, J. (2018). *Advanced facilitator participant workbook*. Freedom, CA: Six Seconds Emotional Intelligence Press.

Freedman, J. (2007). At the heart of leadership. *How to get results with emotional intelligence.* San Mateo: SixSeconds.

Freedman, J. & Roitman, N. (2019). *The EQ gym workbook: Your 6-week workout to put emotional intelligence into action at work and for life*. Freedom, CA: Six Seconds Emotional Intelligence Press.

REFERENCES

Freedman, J. (2007). The physics of emotion: Candace pert on feeling go (o) d. Retrieved from https://www.6seconds.org/2007/01/26/the-physics-of-emotion-candace-pert-on-feeling-good/

Godman, H. (2013, March 06). *Your well-being: more than just a state of mind*. Harvard Health Publishing. Retrieved from https://www.health.harvard.edu/blog/your-well-being-more-than-just-a-state-of-mind-201303065957

Goleman, D. (2014). *What makes a leader: Why emotional intelligence matters*. Florence, MA.: More Than Sound, LLC.

Goleman, D. (2007). *Social intelligence: The new science of human relationships*. New York: Bantam Books.

Goleman, D. (1995). *Emotional intelligence*. New York: Bantam.

Gordon, M. (Host). (2019, May 25). What's Your Purpose? Finding A Sense of Meaning In Life Is Linked To Health [Radio broadcast episode]. Retrieved from https://www.npr.org/sections/health-shots/2019/05/25/726695968/whats-your-purpose-finding-a-sense-of-meaning-in-life-is-linked-to-health

Gordon, T. (2003). Teacher effectiveness training. New York: Three Rivers Press.

Gray, A. (2016, January). The 10 skills you need to thrive in the Fourth Industrial Revolution. In *World Economic Forum* (Vol. 19).

Gyurak, A., Gross, J. J., & Etkin, A. (2011). Explicit and implicit emotion regulation: a dual-process framework. *Cognition and emotion*, 25(3), 400-412.

Iacoboni, M. (2009). Imitation, empathy, and mirror neurons. Annual review of psychology, 60, 653-670.

ICIMS. (2019). The soft skills job seekers need now. Retrieved from https://www.icims.com/hiring-insights/for-employers/the-soft-skills-job-seekers-need-now

Jeffers, S. (2007). *Feel the fear and do it anyway*. New York: Ballantine.

Jensen, A. (2017, January 23). Not just smart goals, setting clear goals for success. *Six Seconds*. Retrieved from https://www.6seconds.org/2017/01/23/emotional-intelligence-in-goal-setting/

Johnson, L. D. (2020). Social-emotional learning in higher education: A program evaluation. Retrieved from https://digitalcommons.nl.edu/diss/455

REFERENCES

Jorgensen, M. & Henretig, J. (2006). eMotion cards. Six Seconds.

Kaufman, S. B., & Jauk, E. (2020). Healthy Selfishness and Pathological Altruism: Measuring Two Paradoxical Forms of Selfishness. *Frontiers in Psychology, 11*, 1006.

Kay, K., & Shipman, C. (2014). The confidence code. *The science and art of self*. NY: HarperCollins.

Kinderman, P., Schwannauer, M., Pontin, E., & Tai, S. (2013). Psychological processes mediate the impact of familial risk, social circumstances and life events on mental health. *PloS one, 8*(10).

Lynn, A., B. (2008). *The eq interview: Finding employees with high emotional intelligence*. New York: American Management Association.

Magicon (2018). *Man* [Online Image]. Retrieved from http://www.projectnoun.com

McGonigal, K. (2016). *The upside of stress: Why stress is good for you, and how to get good at it*. Penguin.

Mehrabian, A. (2008). Communication without words. Communication theory, 6, 193-200.

Miller, M. (2019). The secret to a long life? A meaningful reason to keep living. Six Seconds. Retrieved from https://www.6seconds.org/2019/10/08/the-secret-to-a-long-life-a-meaningful-reason-to-keep-living/

Miller, M. (2018). Injured, alone and afraid: Decision making in the wilderness [memoir]. Six Seconds.

Neely, M. E., Schallert, D. L., Mohammed, S. S., Roberts, R. M., & Chen, Y. J. (2009). Self-kindness when facing stress: The role of self-compassion, goal regulation, and support in college students' well-being. *Motivation and Emotion, 33*(1), 88-97.

Parker, J. D. A., Taylor, R. N., Keefer, K.V., & Summerfeldt, L.J. (2018). Emotional intelligence and post-secondary education: What have we learned and what have we missed? In Keefer, V. K., Parker, J. D. A., & Saklofske, D. H. (Eds.) *Emotional intelligence in education* (pp. 428-452). Cham, Switzerland: Springer.

Plutchik, R. (1982). A psychoevolutionary theory of emotions.

Poh Lin, H. (2019). *Man* [Online image]. Retrieved from http://projectnoun.com

Rasmussen, H. N., Scheier, M. F., & Greenhouse, J. B. (2009). Optimism and physical health: A meta-analytic review. *Annals of behavioral medicine, 37*(3), 239-256.

REFERENCES

Scott, E. (2020, January 29). *The many benefits of optimism*. Verywell Mind. https://www.verywellmind.com/the-benefits-of-optimism-3144811

Seligman, M. E. (2006). *Learned optimism: How to change your mind and your life*. Vintage.

Shapiro, D. (2017). *Negotiating the nonnegotiable: How to resolve your most emotionally charged conflicts*. Penguin.

Shlain, A. (2017a). *Puzzle* [Online Image]. Retrieved from http://www.projectnoun.com

Sjöberg, L. (2001). Emotional intelligence and life adjustment: A validation study. *Sweden: Center for Economic Psychology Stockholm School of Economics*, 1-14.

Smith, S. M., & Krajbich, I. (2019). Gaze amplifies value in decision making. *Psychological science*, *30*(1), 116-128.

Stress tolerance. In *American Psychology Association dictionary*. Retrieved from https://dictionary.apa.org/stress-tolerance

Substance Abuse and Mental Health Services Administration. (2019). *Key substance use and mental health indicators in the United States: Results from the 2018 National Survey on Drug Use and Health* (HHS Publication No. PEP19-5068, NSDUH Series H-54). Rockville, MD: Center for Behavioral Health Statistics and Quality, Substance Abuse and Mental Health Services Administration. Retrieved from https://www.samhsa.gov/data/

University of Texas at Austin. (2011, March 24). Psychologists find the meaning of aggression: 'Monty Python' scene helps research. *ScienceDaily*. Retrieved from www.sciencedaily.com/releases/2011/03/110323105202.htm

Waldinger, R. (2015, June). What makes a good life? Lessons from the longest study on happiness [Video file]. Retrieved from https://www.ted.com/talks/robert_waldinger_what_makes_a_good_life_lessons_from_the_longest_study_on_happiness

Zeidner, M., & Matthews, G. (2018). Grace under pressure in educational contexts: Emotional intelligence, stress, and coping. In K. V. Keefer, J. D. A. Parker, & D. H. Parker (Eds.), *Emotional intelligence in education* (pp. 83-110). Cham, Switzerland: Springer.

GRATITUDE JOURNAL ENTRY

Date: _____/_____/_____

GRATITUDE JOURNAL ENTRY

Date: _____/_____/_____

GRATITUDE JOURNAL ENTRY

Date: ____/____/____

sleep	stethoscope
courtney	tattoos
food	red
chocolate	whitenails
music	Ben + Jerry
school	Bomboocur
nursing	Gymshals

GRATITUDE JOURNAL ENTRY

Date: _____/_____/_____

GRATITUDE JOURNAL ENTRY

Date: _____/_____/_____

GRATITUDE JOURNAL ENTRY

Date: _____/_____/_____

GRATITUDE JOURNAL ENTRY

Date: _____/_____/_____